What people are saying about …

The Slow Fade

"I love twentysomethings and I believe in twentysomethings, which is why I love and believe in this book. We need to do everything within our power to reach the next generation. This book will help you do just that."

Mark Batterson, lead pastor of National
Community Church and author of *Primal*

"If I could, I would *pay* you to read this book. The three voices behind *The Slow Fade* implore us to see the turbulent years facing our twentysomethings and to respond in our churches with an authentic, highly relational ministry that keeps them connected to Jesus. These 'gap years' often result in a disconnect from the church in the midst of questions, culture, pain, and disillusionment. We need to be there with them; this book tells us how."

Nancy Ortberg, speaker and author of
Unleashing the Power of Rubber Bands

"*The Slow Fade* makes us slow down to reflect on what we must do to prevent a slow death from the appalling blood-loss of college students in the body of Christ."

Leonard Sweet, Drew University, George
Fox Evangelical Seminary, sermons.com

"What Joiner, Smith, and Bomar so skillfully communicate in a little less than two hundred pages will likely revolutionize the way you do ministry with college students and young adults. Both well researched and heartfelt, *The Slow Fade* will empower you and your community to make effective and lasting movements toward the very people the church finds hardest to reach. And, perhaps best of all, you will discover how to do this regardless of how small your budget, your congregation, or your vision for how to reach eighteen- to thirty-year-olds."

Jesse Rice, author of *The Church of Facebook*

"College students make incredibly significant decisions and ask profoundly impactful questions as they transition into adulthood; to walk alone is a recipe for disaster. If everyone followed the personal and practical solutions offered in *The Slow Fade,* we would see a dramatic change in the landscape of our churches."

Aaron Stern, college pastor of theMILL at New Life Church

THE
SLOW FADE

WHY YOU MATTER IN THE
STORY OF TWENTYSOMETHINGS

THE
SLOW FADE

REGGIE JOINER
CHUCK BOMAR
& ABBIE SMITH

David C Cook®
transforming lives together

THE SLOW FADE
Published by David C. Cook
4050 Lee Vance View
Colorado Springs, CO 80918 U.S.A.

David C. Cook Distribution Canada
55 Woodslee Avenue, Paris, Ontario, Canada N3L 3E5

David C. Cook U.K., Kingsway Communications
Eastbourne, East Sussex BN23 6NT, England

David C. Cook and the graphic circle C logo
are registered trademarks of Cook Communications Ministries.

The Web site addresses recommended throughout this book are offered as a
resource to you. These Web sites are not intended in any way to be or imply an
endorsement on the part of David C. Cook, nor do we vouch for their content.

Scripture quotations marked NIV are taken from the *Holy Bible, New International
Version*. *NIV*. Copyright © 1973, 1978, 1984 International Bible Society. Used
by permission of Zondervan. All rights reserved. Scripture quotations marked MSG
are taken from *THE MESSAGE*. Copyright © by Eugene H. Peterson 1993, 1994,
1995, 1996, 2000, 2001, 2002. Used by permission of NavPress Publishing Group.
Scripture quotations marked NASB are taken from the *New American Standard Bible*,
© Copyright 1960, 1995 by The Lockman Foundation. Used by permission.

LCCN 2010922111
ISBN 978-1-4347-6479-9
eISBN 978-0-7814-0439-6

© 2010 Reggie Joiner, Abbie Smith, and Chuck Bomar
Published in association with the literary agency of
D.C. Jacobson & Associates LLC, an Authors Management Company
www.dcjacobson.com

The David C. Cook Team: Don Pape, Caitlyn York,
Amy Kiechlin, Sarah Schultz, Karen Athen
The reThink Team: Jared Herd, Kristen Ivy, Mike Jeffries,
Hannah Joiner, Beth Nelson, and Tim Walker
Cover design: Studio Gearbox

Printed in the United States of America
First Edition 2010

1 2 3 4 5 6 7 8 9 10

022610

Reggie Joiner—

To those who have invested in the lives of my children, Reggie Paul, Hannah, Rebekah, and Sarah: each of you has left a powerful imprint that has helped shape our family.

Chuck Bomar—

To Ron Wilson: Thanks for decades of faithfully investing in younger people. You are a great example for all to follow.

Abbie Smith—

To Kim, Erin, and Sister Julia: Thank you for caring about college students. Your investment in my life finds me eternally grateful.

Contents

Acknowledgments

Jared Herd, Kristen Ivy, Mike Jeffries, Hannah Joiner, Beth Nelson, and Tim Walker: Thanks for all the hours you spent with us providing your wisdom and insight.

A Note to the Reader

Three distinct voices have combined to create *The Slow Fade.* These chapters are written from each of the authors' unique perspectives, and their voices provide different viewpoints for examining the fade.

Reggie Joiner

I sensed the fade twenty years ago.

In many ways, we started North Point Community Church because of it. I began to witness this age group's drift away from faith as a young pastor, and when I invested in a few college-aged people, I recognized the change that was occurring within myself. I was fascinated by them. Encouraged by them. Committed to them. As my four children grew, my desire for strong voices in their lives became even more significant. My voice in the coming pages represents not only decades of work as a pastor but decades of parenting.

Chuck Bomar

I started fighting the fade more than ten years ago.

I led the student and university ministry at Cornerstone Church in Simi Valley for eight and a half years before moving to Portland, Oregon, to start Colossae. My desire is to help every church in every context embrace ministry to college-aged people as vital, recognizing that one of the biggest challenges facing churches today is the loss of young people. And we church leaders have no one to blame but ourselves. My voice in this book is the product of years of ministry work with college-aged people.

Abbie Smith

I am experiencing the fade.

Well, perhaps four years removed—given our loosely held parameters of ages eighteen to twenty-five—but close enough. I'm a believing twentysomething, wrestling with how I fit into life's tapestry. I started following Jesus somewhere around my freshman year at Emory University, and I became quickly impassioned by the story of God and what it meant that I had a story therein. By my senior year, I had compiled a book, sharing stories from students around the country about their faith journeys in college.[1] Since then I have worked alongside various collegiate ministries and movements, stateside and abroad, and recently completed a graduate degree in spiritual formation and soul care at Talbot Seminary. My voice in these pages hopes to represent one near enough to the fading population to see inside it, while removed enough to see perspectives from the outside.

Chapter 1

The Invisible Years

A few years ago I (Reggie) went to a salon to get my hair cut (and if you know me, you know my time in the chair to get a trim goes pretty fast). I struck up a conversation with the college-aged guy named Rick they assigned to me. He was an open book. In the fifteen minutes it took to cut my hair, he told me about the town where he had grown up, his involvement as a teenager with a large church, his struggle getting along with his dad, his two-year attempt at getting a college degree from the University of Georgia, the girl he had moved in with, his intrigue with Scientology, and his disillusionment with Christianity. Over the next few months we had fascinating conversations about his perspectives and worldview. He admitted that the turning point for him had been his first years of college. His parents had connected him to a local church in his college town that one of their adult friends had recommended. The first Sunday he showed up, the pastor was in the middle of a series about the "danger of Halloween and the occult." One of the older men in the church invited him to their Monday morning men's prayer breakfast. Other than a card in the mail inviting him to a college social, he said he felt like the church just wasn't designed for his stage of life. He didn't fit in; he even said he felt somewhat invisible. The following week, he began a unit of study in his sociology class on comparative religions. He mentioned how highly intelligent and inspiring his professor was and how the class gave him an opportunity to process questions he had been struggling with for years.

His first year of college was the last time he ever went to church.

Various versions of Rick's story have been repeated in my life countless times. I run into twentysomethings everywhere I go—

The waitress who was raised by a Christian family

The intern who grew up in church youth group and is now active in a political campaign

The coffee shop manager who was an FCA leader in high school

The photographer who went on the annual church mission trip to Mexico

These are real friends of mine. And the one thing they have in common is they all are becoming disconnected from their communities of faith. At a time in their lives when their faith should be accelerating, it has begun to dim. At a stage when they're developing a new network of friends, there is a relational gap. At the moment they are beginning to wrestle with what they thought was certain, they are missing voices they know they can trust.

They are fading off the radar of those who were their Christian leaders during the very season when they are trying to solidify what they really believe.

It is not intentional on anyone's part. No one is deliberately orchestrating the fade. It is just out of sight, out of mind. And some of the most influential and promising leaders of faith for the next generation are being ignored and gradually fading from view.

If you are reading this book, you probably have children who are college-aged, or you care about someone who is. Or maybe someone who has college-aged children or friends gave you this book because they are hoping to get you to think about that group of people. College-aged people are all around you, but are you noticing them? To some, they are an enigma—kind of like ghosts drifting in and out of your world, invisible until they are given their adult roles, at which time they become "real people." It's like they fade out of high school and then fade back into adulthood, and for a few years we just assume they are transforming into mature adults.

Until a few years ago the college-aged person was invisible to the political community, too, but then something changed. Regardless of what you think about Barack Obama's presidential campaign, it proved something in the history of politics: College-aged people matter! Not only did this demographic's vote count, it added incredible momentum to the campaign. Both Democrat and Republican leaders had dismissed eighteen- to twenty-five-year-olds as a group who never really turned out for elections. No one took them seriously … until after the election. Then the numbers made it obvious they had made a difference in the presidential election of 2008.

The young voter turnout tripled or even quadrupled in the last election. More than 6.5 million young voters participated in the primary contests or caucuses in 2008, an increase of 103 percent over the same statistic in 2004.[2]

The political community may never view eighteen- to twenty-five-year-olds the same way it did before 2008. Skeptics ignored the rise in voter registrations from this age group and suggested they were unlikely to show up. Obama's campaign targeted this age group with an attitude that suggested they could make a difference in who would be elected president—and they did.

Savvy organizations look for ways to harness the energy of twentysomethings. Any entity that ignores this age group's potential runs the risk of becoming outdated and irrelevant. The principle is simple: It is difficult to sustain influence with culture if you lose your influence with the college-aged person. The lesson the political community taught us about the influence of this group is valuable for all who live in the faith community. If we who are living in the Christian adult world don't begin to see the college-aged person in a different way, we will continue to contribute to what we call the slow fade.

Slow Fade

Research indicates there is a slow fade occurring with respect to many people's level of involvement in today's church. An obvious decline is evident when you trace their activity within the local church from the time they are born until their first few years of college. The line rises in preschool and begins to fall at middle school. It dips in the later high school years and then nose-dives the first years of college. Every expert suggests the same thing—somewhere between 65 and 80 percent of people who grow up in the church drop out of church when they become college-aged.

An America's Research Group survey conducted in 2009 found that 95 percent of twenty- to twenty-nine-year-old evangelicals attended church regularly during their elementary and middle school years, but only 55 percent attended during high school. By the time they reached college, only 11 percent were still attending church.[3]

Losing Faith

More important than what seems to be happening in church attendance is what seems to be happening to the faith of this age group. Several years ago, David Kinnaman, now the president of Barna Research, pointed this out:

> There is considerable debate about whether the disengagement of twentysomethings is a lifestage issue—that is, a predictable element in the progression of people's development as they go through various family, occupational and chronological stages—or whether it is unique to this generation. While there is some

truth to both explanations, this debate misses the point, which is that the current state of ministry to twentysomethings is woefully inadequate to address the spiritual needs of millions of young adults. These individuals are making significant life choices and determining the patterns and preferences of their spiritual reality while churches wait, generally in vain, for them to return after college or when the kids come. When and if young adults do return to churches, it is difficult to convince them that a passionate pursuit of Christ is anything more than a nice add-on to their cluttered lifestyle.[4]

The trend of eighteen- to twenty-five-year-olds disengaging from church and faith has been a growing problem for more than twenty years. While those who are college-aged are increasingly fading out of the picture, mainstream denominations and independent churches are slowly graying and declining in attendance. The sad news is that churches' strategies to reach these twentysomethings have not significantly adjusted to respond to this issue. When you ask the average church what their plan is for college-aged people, you usually get confused looks. Frankly, twentysomethings are perceived by most leaders in churches as a transient demographic, people who don't tithe and who need to solidify their faith on their own.

As the new college minister at a church located just blocks from one of the nation's most prestigious northeastern schools, a friend of mine was brought onto the staff to do intentional campus outreach. His first day on the job, he went to the youth minister to ask for the names of the church's recent graduates, their addresses, and their current universities or colleges if they were enrolled in higher education. He wanted to make follow-up calls to see how they were transitioning and if the church body could assist them in any way. My friend's question was met with a look of bewilderment. "Why would I have that information?" the youth minister said. "They've already graduated."

Most churches and families have programmed a finish line in youth or student ministry at twelfth grade. At church we push our seniors out the door, breathe a sigh of relief, and let them disappear for a few years. There is a mistaken assumption that they will spend the next four or five years solidifying their faith, starting careers, getting married, and showing back up at our churches when they are more "complete" adults. So we let them go ... because that is what we are supposed to do, right?

What if we have drawn the wrong finish line?

What if the relational connection is more important in college than it ever was in high school?

What if the decisions they are about to make are some of the most critical choices of their lives?

What if we have allowed them to become invisible when we should be even more actively involved with their worlds?

Consider the following ideas from Kristen Ivy, one of our XP3 curriculum editors, from a research project she did in seminary:

> Disconnection from the community during late adolescence isolates them precisely during what are considered "critical years." Derek Melleby from the CPYU College Transition Initiative says, "Decisions are made during this time that are formative for the rest of life." A study from the Fuller Youth Institute has found that "one noticeable and consistent trend" for late adolescents is "that higher-risk behaviors are correlated with lower faith integration." If someone does not become intentional about reaching out to this group of transitioning adolescents, they are left to make these decisions without the accountability of community or the wisdom of those who may have seen and experienced more in life than they. On the other hand, when church community is present during the period of late adolescence it is also transformational. The most recent studies from LifeWay Research show that "among young adults ages twenty-three to thirty *who stayed in church during ages eighteen to twenty-two*, only 6 percent do not currently attend church.[5]

Moving the Line

For the past several years, hosts of leaders and ministers, including those who are partners with us in the Orange initiatives, have wrestled with issues related to the slow fade occurring in the next generation. We have encouraged countless churches to rethink and redesign how they do ministry to kids and teenagers. There has been a new emphasis on critical shifts that need to happen in order to effectively influence the next generation. In the book *Think Orange,* we give an exhaustive explanation of the five critical issues that will help churches and families become more effective in transferring faith to kids and students. In this book, we want to highlight what may be one of the most critical decisions a church or family can make related to its strategy: Move the finish line from twelfth grade to the age of college graduation.

I know what you are thinking: Is there ever really a finish line? No, but there is a clear moment when late adolescence transitions to adulthood, and not one expert says it happens at high school graduation. The problem is that in the average church ministry and family, we have been programmed to let go when these students graduate instead of transitioning them relationally. Giving the right focus to those who are college-aged has to become a priority for Christian leaders and parents.

If you are a strategic thinker or smart businessperson, it makes sense to protect the investment you have made through multiple years of influence in someone's life. Think about it for just a moment: If the slow fade in someone's faith begins to occur at the point he or she goes off to college, then why don't we focus some of our best energies on the first few years of college? If you stop at high school graduation, you stop short of the finish line.

If you played baseball as a child, think about the shift from Little League to Pony League. Everything changed just enough to throw off your game. The most noticeable difference was the distance between the bases. If you were a Little League veteran, it felt like someone moved the finish line. Some of us were embarrassed when we started our slide too soon and stopped short of the bag. The extra distance required a critical adjustment. Your brain and legs had been programmed for a sixty-foot run. Coaches made you practice sliding so you could develop a sense of timing. The repetition enabled your instincts to take over and send your legs into a slide right into the edge of the bag. But just when you were getting the hang of it, they changed the rules. They moved the base thirty feet farther away. In order to master the extra distance, you now had to unlearn what your body was programmed to do. Regardless of how well you hit the ball or how hard you ran, if you stopped short of the bag, it was all in vain. You were out.

Church leaders and parents have been programmed for decades to make an eighteen-year run. Then we pick up the adults after college and get them to plug into their adult careers and adult church programs. This is a pivotal moment for leaders. Over the past several decades, someone has changed the distance between the bases, and we need to consider reprogramming our brains to go an extra few years. When it comes to transitioning people into an adult world with a maturing faith, we are stopping the strategy too soon.

So what's the answer? How can we affect the slow fade in a positive way? How can we influence the faith of college students during the critical years of the faith? How can we continue to build on the investment we have had in so many kids who have grown up in our homes and churches? Is the answer simply to create more effective college ministry programs? Are we suggesting there should be a new breed of college ministries established in churches all across the country? Not really. The issue is not to reinvent college ministry in the local church, or this book would have simply been written to church staffs or student pastors. Although there are some principles here that translate for the local church, our desire in writing this is to appeal to a different audience.

If you are an adult who is interested in influencing the slow fade, we hope this book will mobilize you to build a relationship with someone who is college-aged.

The real question is, who has the greatest potential to influence the faith of those who are in their late teens and twenties? Yes, we think it is the church, but more specifically Christian adults who are *in* the church who have a passion to invest in this age group.

The strategy is simple: Recruit a new breed of mentors to invest time in those who are college-aged.

Don't let the word *mentor* scare you; it's not as hard as it sounds. (We will discuss it more in later chapters.) For now, we need you to understand that intentional time invested in someone during this critical transitional period could make a significant difference in the direction of that person's life.

I love to poke around and ask questions to college students to understand more about their worlds and their issues. Recently I was talking with a group of college interns, and I asked why most of them had not connected with a church in their area. One girl immediately said, "It's just too hard." When I asked her what she meant by "hard" she replied, "In my first year of college, everything was new and changing. I had to figure out where my classes were, what my major was, find new friends, start living off a budget, search for a job.… Trying to figure out where to go to church was just too hard. I tried once, but I didn't really connect with anyone." I have repeated that conversation a number of times, and the responses usually come back to a variety of reasons, most of which are related to the difficulty college-aged people have in finding a community of faith where they belong and are able to connect.

Kristen, our XP3 editor who also happens to be a volunteer small-group leader at her church, tried an experiment recently. Since she leads high school girls, she has seen a couple of twelfth-grade groups graduate. The system encourages volunteers to lead a group of girls or guys for a few years to build a trusted relationship, but graduation had always marked the finish line of the service as a small-group leader. After that, many would start the process again with a ninth-grade group.

But for some reason the transition didn't feel right to Kristen. She was worried about the slow fade. Even though the church prepared a good-bye, served a graduation dinner, and handed her a gift card as a sign of gratitude for her four years of leadership, she felt like her time with this group was still incomplete. After talking with the youth minister, she decided to commit to an extra year with her group. Some of the girls were still living at home and had jobs in her area. Some of the girls had gone to local universities, and others were in private and public schools around the country. They no longer met weekly, but she stayed committed to pursuing a relationship with them. One semester she visited each of their college campuses within driving distance to spend time with the girls in their new environments. She set up a time each week to send messages on Facebook to connect with and encourage them. When the girls were home on holidays, she planned a few coffee and dinner meetings. Over Christmas break, they had a reunion sleepover that was the group's most well-attended event in five years. Part of her commitment to this group of girls included replacing herself. The goal of her continued commitment was not to hold on indefinitely but to love them through this crucial transition time and help them take the next step in their faith journeys. She had gone with them to a local college ministry, since there wasn't one at their home church, and she regularly checked in with them to get a feel for whether they were finding other leaders in their new locations. For those who were still at home, she looked for ways to connect them to service opportunities at their church where they could meet other young adults and experience true community.

Some of what she did during that first college year was systematic, but most of it was organic. All the girls experienced transition in their own unique ways, and the way Kristen pursued them and the amount of time she spent with them depended a lot on the individual situation. Kristen discovered that the life experiences of the girls in college became more critical. During their first year out of high school, one girl's mother went into the hospital. One girl's sister died. Another experienced a major turnover in her parents' church. Another girl's parents got divorced while she was in college. Kristen made some important discoveries during her relationships with these girls in this time, and in a number of scenarios the quality of her conversations went deeper than they ever went in high school.

She concluded that all church leaders who work with youth should take a look at the systems they have for graduating seniors. Even when they have officially checked out of the youth program, many seniors are still relationally present. She realized that there is a critical need—one that has been overlooked.

There is a critical need for adults to connect relationally with those who are college-aged.

Someone who will become a trusted voice of encouragement and reason.

Someone who recognizes that the college years have a defining nature.

Someone who will help them transition from late adolescence to adulthood.

After walking with Kristen through the transition of her group into college, our staff recognized two critical things:

1. We are disconnecting from teenagers at graduation, when the stakes are the highest.

2. We are not tapping into our relational influence, when the felt need is the greatest.

With all the growing statistics about the church drop-off rate for college freshmen and young adults, we need to reevaluate how we connect with this generation. What would happen if adults and leaders decided that graduation simply wasn't the finish line?

A Parent's Plea

At the time this book will be released, my children will be twenty-five, twenty-three, twenty-one, and nineteen years old. I am more convinced than ever that the leaders who have invested in my son and daughters during their elementary and teenage years have had critical influence. Those were important years that have affected their concept of God. There are countless stories and faces of the people who have influenced their faith and molded their views, people who will be lifelong friends to them.

As important as their teenage years were, this stage is different. The stakes are extremely high. Over the past couple of years I have watched my kids struggle with college and career choices, establish new friends, move into their own spaces, move back home again, date, and in a couple of situations go through heartbreaking situations that emptied them emotionally. The one thing I am most grateful for during this phase is the adult men and women who invest in my children's lives. I am smart enough to know that I am not the only leader they need to help them navigate these years. I decided a long time ago to look for opportunities to encourage them to connect with mentors and leaders our family could trust to be wise voices in their worlds.

At some point in my life I realized I should be involved in doing the same thing I hoped other people would do for my children. I have watched college-aged people wait tables, manage retail stores, hang out at movie theaters and coffee shops, and I've seen they are almost always with their peers. It seems like they disappear in the eyes of the adult population that walks by them or orders from them or sits next to them.

Something has changed in me over the past decade when I see someone in this age bracket. When I meet someone who is college-aged, I think about my kids, then I think about their parents, and I wonder what I can do that would reflect what I would want another adult to do if this were my son or daughter. It's not that I am extremely gracious or noble; it's just that I am a dad and I have children, and I know adults who care about my kids. So I tend to care about other people's kids; it's just contagious that way. I have this tendency to tell every adult I meet to consider investing in someone who is college-aged. When I meet twentysomethings, I can't help thinking, *Who is the adult in your world who really cares about you, who is willing to connect with you in a healthy way?*

The church will continue to struggle with ways to implement a more strategic ministry for this age group. But as Christian adults, you and I don't have to wait for the church to figure this out and have a better plan. You can start today to influence a college-aged person. The best way to stop the slow fade in the next generation is to stop it in one person's life.

Chapter 2

Personal Epic

As I (Abbie) stared down at my journal, the words *lonely, void,* and *confused* stared back. It was the summer after my high school graduation, and I knew something had to change. I'd been raised in a loving family, though, and I was thrilled to be heading off to college, so where was this desperation coming from? And why was it gnawing away at me? At the time, I couldn't put a finger on it, but now it's clear that much of my plight revolved around lacking relationship with and searching for God.

Overall, my childhood was positive, and unlike most, it seems, my middle school and high school experiences were relatively enjoyable. I had parents who raised me with care and pointed me toward a prosperous life. So on the outside, I was put together and well rounded, leaving for college to pursue dreams of playing tennis and majoring in psychology. But on the inside, I was empty and afraid. I was like the chocolate bunnies grandmothers send at Easter—solid and ravishing in its outer shell, but with one bite, found to be fragile and devastatingly empty.

"How can I ask for more, though?" I questioned. "And even if I do, where would I begin my search?" The world had given me everything—great friends, a loving family, and an exciting life ahead of me. Plus, college was supposed to be the best four years of my life, right? And yet here I was at the fragile age of eighteen, scared of leaving home and disillusioned by the thought of losing every framework my world had ever known.

Maybe it makes sense, then, that crossing paths with a handful of more sturdy individuals those early weeks of my freshman year was highly meaningful. Not sturdy in the sense of perfect, perfectly put together, or perfected in all their answers, but sturdy in the sense of knowing *why* and *for what end* they existed—and living their lives accordingly. Sturdy in the sense of knowing they were loved by God and invited into God's story. Awestruck to find others my age living for a purpose and within a story more compelling than any I'd ever heard, I wanted the same. So as I was introduced to Jesus through a variety of avenues that freshman year, I realized that I, too, could engage with such an unheard-of story. I said yes.

Questions arose quickly, though. What might it look like to be in a sorority or play on a sports team *as a Christian?* Or how was I to deal with professors whose lessons conflicted with what I was hearing on Sunday mornings, whose paradigms were antithetical to those I grew up with? My college was a small liberal arts school with about a hundred active Christians in a mix of five thousand, so my community of peers was certainly instrumental—even crucial—at times. I was experiencing new levels of acceptance and growth through spending time with those in my same season of life. But it wasn't long before I wanted more. Looking back, it was the influence of a few willing adults during my college years that ultimately changed my life.

Transforming Roles

First, there was Kim. She and her husband were campus ministers who spent their lives investing in college students. New to this Jesus stuff, I found the concept of that job really weird in some ways, especially when I bounced it off my parents (who thought I'd joined a cult) or high school friends (who thought I must have started doing drugs). In other ways, though, the concept of such a job was one of the most intriguing things I'd ever heard. These people liked God and believed in the potential of college students so much that they were investing their entire lives toward those ends. Kim said she'd love to get to know me more and asked if I'd ever want to hang out. No adult had ever asked me such a thing. I was so honored and amazed and intrigued that someone like her, surely a busy mom and wife, would want to hang out with *me*. We met in my dorm room that freshman year. She talked some but probably listened more. I don't remember many of her answers to my questions or the names of any books we read together. What I remember is the tingly feeling I got the first time she asked if she could pray for me and how it felt to have someone believe in me before I knew how to believe in myself.

Erin was another woman who influenced me immensely. I met her at a church I had starting attending my sophomore year, and she, too, seemed far less interested in my talents, résumé, or successes as she did simply in *me*. Erin's vulnerability was one of the most refreshing things about her. She had an obvious dependence on God, but she wasn't afraid to admit her struggles and even show them to me up close. One night we were sitting in her living room after she had gone through a recent breakup. It was cold outside, and we made chocolate chip cookies. I remember not understanding why at the time but knowing that it meant a lot when she cried in front of me.

One afternoon while working on this book, I received a letter from a final woman I'd like to introduce—an eighty-year-old nun. I met Sister Julia while at a retreat center. Fascinated by the thought of spending time with someone who'd followed God for more years than I had lived, I asked if she'd ever be willing to sit down with me. She seemed honored. We had a chance to be face-to-face only a few times, but those few times will impact me for a lifetime. Sister Julia didn't need to speak my twentysomething language or live in the world of Facebook, exams, and *The Office* to have a profound effect on me. And the way she related to me spurred my relations with another generation. Her interest in my story and her fascination with who I was forced me to reconsider the stories of others. Maybe they, too, were valued creatures at a given stage in God's story, worth my fascination.

I can honestly say these women paved the way for much of who I am today. They were my references for the life of a godly woman, far beyond that of a Bible study or series on Song of Solomon. They gave me a tangible experience and witness of learning to follow Jesus—as a wife, friend, woman, mom, and human. They let me into their walks with God—into weakness and longing, hope and spiritual disciplines. Sometimes I related to stuff any one of them would say, but probably more times I didn't. It didn't matter, though, because for a given amount of time, I got to be a little girl, watching from the heels of a woman. I got to be an adult who drank coffee and talked about marriage and God and politics. I got to be the one whose dreams were listened to and whose doubts were held. And in the most practical of terms, I got to be cared for in my adolescence while being caringly invited into adulthood. I got to belong.

One Issue, One Thousand Ways

To know that we belong—ultimately to God—is arguably the end we were made for and the beginning of being made whole. Though acceptance is often an external (or felt) craving, belonging is the layer that lies beneath. Acceptance is fleeting and arbitrary, whereas belonging is grounded in something more permanent. Belonging stems from the knowledge that I am intrinsically connected to a place, or people, beyond myself. I can dress stylishly, speak eloquently, or excel at something enough to find acceptance. But my acceptance will always be based on something *about me*—and thus up for grabs when that something changes or falls short. What I need is to be loved based on simply being *me*.

College-aged people don't cut themselves, suffer from eating disorders, change majors seven times, change churches ten times, or abandon church altogether because they're flighty. They do so because they don't know where they belong. If I don't know why I belong to something, or how I bring unity to that something to some degree, there's little reason to stick around.

The searches flesh out in a thousand different ways. Whether it's becoming a vegetarian, sleeping around, rallying for a campaign, tattooing an ankle, experimenting with drugs, or fighting to save Darfur, this age-stage in particular portrays external behaviors, or embodiments, of an internal conflict of individuation wondering, "Who am I, and how do I fit into this picture?"

Looking back at my story, I was enmeshed between flamboyant passions to save the world and passionate demands to be treated like an adult. In other words, understanding where I belonged was an absolute anomaly. Some hours I cared about mature things, like politics and saving starving kids in Ethiopia, but other hours I was stuck in unresolved pains of a breakup, or I needed help figuring out life away from home. In so many ways, I was trapped between worlds and simply needed someone to reach in and validate my existence.

When I boil it down, though, there were really just three questions I was consciously or subconsciously driven by, relating to myself, God, and others, respectively:

1. Who am I?

2. What does it mean to be God's daughter?

3. How do I fit into the world around me?

Unique Categories

I didn't grow up in the church, nor did I have anything of a faith association prior to college. For me, then, belonging in my college years initially revolved around finding my place in God's story. But all people are unique in their needs and attractions, so everyone's search for belonging will look different. The attractions of an eighteen-year-old will be different from those of a twenty-four-year-old. Someone coming from a divorced home or adjusting to the death of a parent will obviously share a different set of searches and pursue different points of belonging.

Consider Phil, who grew up in the church and recently went off to college. He's been an avid church and youth group attendee his whole life. Never having tasted any outward forms of rebellion, Phil is going wild. He wants to experience life outside the walls of the church because he feels suffocated when within. Phil is searching for identity and freedom and a discovery of his voice outside of what he's grown up with.

Or take my friend Danielle, a twenty-year-old who calls herself a "searching agnostic." I'll never forget the night I invited her to join a friend and me for dinner. And mind you, this friend is the type who wears a WWJD bracelet and feels led to ask everyone he meets where they'll go if they die tonight. (Clearly I was just hungry and didn't think through the dining dynamics.) I cringed every time he asked Danielle's thoughts on God or religion. But as she and I stood in the parking lot afterward and I apologized on his behalf, her response shocked me: "Abbie, whether what he's saying is right or wrong is really beside the point for me. I just thought it was neat to be around someone who believed enough in something to hinge his whole life on it." Danielle was craving a sturdy construct of beliefs, and she was open to just about anything in hopes of finding it.

Finally, I'll mention Sean, a twenty-three-year-old lover of God who spends his days working for a nonprofit and his nights busing tables. Sean has no desire to attend college but all the desire in the world to impact God's kingdom. Stories like these could go on and on. But here's what's gripping: Any category will always boil down to a search for belonging in (at least) one of three areas: self, God, and others. *Who am I* as an individual? *Where do I fit* in God's story? And *how can my life make a difference?*

College-aged individuals *will search* for belonging in the world, and the world will make every effort to help them find it. Whether it's a choice between Chi Phi or Sigma Nu, thousands of screaming fans, or newfound freedoms to eat, sleep, be, say, or share beds with whomever, till whenever, wherever, their searching ground is ripe with options—and sexy ones at that. So either we can engage with them and validate their journeys, or we can continue to alienate them and expect the world's enticements and illusions to pick up what we've dropped.

No one ever tires of wanting to be heard or needing a safe space to process life. College-aged people may annoy you, not pick up their Starbucks trash, or act remotely interested in what you're saying. But they are. Often they just don't know how to say so or believe they're worth your time and energy. They don't need an expert, theologian, or fully put-together person to help them find their places. They need someone who cares enough about their stories to listen as they process, validate as they search, and unite with them as they journey toward God and adulthood.

But I also want you to think about how this keeps your significance from getting blown up into self-

importance. For no matter how significant you are, it is only because of what you are a part of. An enormous eye or a gigantic hand wouldn't be a body, but a monster. What we have is one body with many parts, each its proper size and in its proper place. No part is important on its own. Can you imagine Eye telling Hand, "Get lost; I don't need you"? Or, Head telling Foot, "You're fired; your job has been phased out"? As a matter of fact, in practice it works the other way— the "lower" the part, the more basic, and therefore necessary. You can live without an eye, for instance, but not without a stomach. When it's a part of your own body you are concerned with, it makes no difference whether the part is visible or clothed, higher or lower. You give it dignity and honor just as it is, without comparisons. If anything, you have more concern for the lower parts than the higher. If you had to choose, wouldn't you prefer good digestion to full-bodied hair?

—1 Corinthians 12:19–24 (MSG)

Chapter 3

Common Ground

When we read stories like Abbie's, we realize the impact one person can have on another. It's inspiring because we all have those people in our lives who have left a positive mark on us. And some of them don't even know they did. They just spent time with us or said one thing that somehow stuck all these years. And deep down, we would all love to be that person for someone else.

So what do we do? What are the practical next steps for coming alongside college-aged people and positively influencing them in the same way?

Well, believe it or not, we're going to say you shouldn't *do* anything. Yes, nothing.

Because before we start thinking outwardly, we need to look inwardly. Over the course of the next few chapters, we'll discuss the issues college-aged people are facing and how you can come alongside them in that process. But first, there's a commonality in Abbie's story mirroring each of our own that we must pay attention to. There are questions of identity, belonging, and worth that we all wrestle with, questions we seek to resolve in our own stories. So answering these questions for ourselves is where we must start.

Our goal here isn't to put you through a psychological biopsy. It's simply to bring out the fact that each of us is still in process. Regardless of where we are in life, there is a longing for something more than what we currently have. We can look back on some parts of our pasts with feelings of gratitude, yet other parts give rise to feelings of regret. We're glad we held on to some things over the years, but others we wish we'd never lost. And it's those lost things that need to be recaptured.

Though they may seem insignificant, they're incredibly crucial.

Recapturing Wonder

I (Chuck) have two daughters: Karis and Hope. Having children is obviously an amazing thing for many different reasons. Of course, I appreciate and savor some aspects of parenting more than others. One of my least favorite aspects is seeing my own negative characteristics come out in my kids. That is frustrating. On the other hand, one of my favorite things is watching them play, especially when they don't know I'm doing so.

I'm fascinated by the conversations they have with the imaginary who-knows-what. I often think about how their minds work, what they're thinking through, and how they can get to that imaginary land so quickly. They can shut out everything else almost automatically. Maybe it's the lack of worry or responsibility that gives them that freedom. Or maybe they just don't take themselves as seriously as we do, and because of that, they have a curiosity that allows for this magical play. Either way, I love peeking in the door and enjoying their little minds' work, even if it's just for a few minutes. Through my relationship with my girls, I get a sense of awe and freedom … and enjoyment.

These glimpses into childlike imagination and wonder can leave us adults wishing we'd never let go of that. Isn't there something inside you that wishes you could go to that place again? A place where all the worry, all the responsibility, and all adultlike appropriateness went out the door for just a little while? It's a place that doesn't make any rational sense to an adult, but every one of us longs for it.

Somehow, this imagination is squelched as we get older. Our sense of wonder and curiosity about life seems to fade with age, and this happens in our faith as well. Deep down, we all know there's something magical and wondrous about the Christian faith—a God who loves us and His Son who died for us—but if we're honest, most Christians get over that early in life, or we push it away from our day-to-day mindsets.

Sure, we have moments that remind us why we believe or why we go to church and make our kids go too. But how often are we moved to a sense of wonder and curiosity about who God is and what He has done? Somewhere along the way, a sense of wonder became a relic of our pasts, tucked away in childhood memories. But recovering this wonder is a necessity in looking toward our hopes for the future.

Some people get nervous when we talk about God being mysterious, or how certain areas of faith aren't as clear as we'd like them to be. But the truth here lies in the wonder-full sides of

God's character—that He is always looking for ways to surprise us. Sometimes what we think we know about Him turns out to be very narrow. Or what we thought He'd do, He doesn't ... or maybe vice versa. God loves people we don't have patience for, and He sees those we don't even know exist. God cares about things we intentionally ignore. He's unpredictable, but He can be known. And yet, there always seems to be more.

These are the things that lead us to acknowledge God for who He is. There are all kinds of things we can't totally grasp, things we can't seem to put a finger on. We don't get how His sense of justice works. We can't come close fathoming all He's up to at any given moment. Our minds can't seem to understand how His full being is never in one spot at any given time. All this to say, we are filled with wonder. And we don't have to go to a magical land where we talk to an imaginary who-knows-what.

God is at the core of this longing we all have. Before we seek to invest in a college-aged person, this sense of wonder needs to be recaptured in our own lives. Even if just for a few brief moments.[6]

Reestablishing Discovery

The college-aged years are filled with discovery for young people, most of which revolves around themselves. It's a time of self-awareness, discovering who they are, how they fit in the world, and what they want to accomplish or be a part of. They are thinking through what commitments they want to shape the rest of their lives. What things will bring them a sense of meaning and purpose?

And yet again, all of this, to some degree, is material we should never stop thinking through.

It's when we discover who we are in God that we discover our purpose and find meaning. When we lose sight of our identities, we lose understanding of our purpose and meaning. And it's the latter loss that happens to most of us.

We chase a career or certain lifestyle and sometimes get there, only to find a temporary sense of satisfaction that dissipates over time. Our wishful thoughts of finding meaning in the things of the world get crushed by reality. And moments like this remind us that the process of discovering who we are never should have ended. Intuitively, each of us knows this. But rarely do we take time for the work that the process demands.

Too many don't want to admit this, but embracing our identity in God is never done. People have suggested that at some point you have to land on who you are and stick with it no matter what. This might be true to a point, but recognizing that we're constantly in process is critical for every believer. And the process is worth it. Life is filled with hurts, disappointments, and challenges that shape who we are, and it's the continued commitment to self-discovery that allows us to grow into who God is shaping us to be.

The choice is always before us. Are we willing to remain teachable and continue moving toward discovery?

Intentionally moving forward in this process is both healthy and necessary as believers, but it is also one of the things that makes us effective with college-aged people. We'll examine this more in the chapters to come.

Unleashing Passion

Passion is that thing that leads us into being part of something bigger than ourselves. It's a unique word that is usually thought of as an emotion, but it actually describes something relational, something seen in ourselves and in other people. We quickly recognize passion in others and are immediately drawn to it. Everyone desires to be around passionate people. It's intriguing and contagious. You can see it on people's faces or hear it in their voices, and when it's recognized, it's pursued.

The problem is, passion can easily become lost as we get older. We can all remember being passionate about something at some point in our lives. Sometimes wisdom tells us these things weren't worth our energy, yet there's still something about that passion we long to feel again. It can be disheartening to recognize that somewhere along the journey of life, we abandoned passion. Or it was hijacked by something that didn't benefit us or the rest of the world. We spend so much of our time in church trying to get it back or feel it again. But the reality is, passion cannot be rescued until we're deeply connected to other passionate people.

One of the first times I (Abbie) sensed lost passion in my life was also the first recognizable time that true passion unleashed itself on me. I was at a point in life where I felt stuck, frustrated, and maybe just bored, or unable to enjoy myself and the place where God had my story. My dad and I were on a trip to South Africa together and en route to a township near Soweto. With us was Gogo, an aged woman by the looks of her worn skin and lack of mobility. But she was a ten-year-old child by the radiance and infective joy of her spirit. Gogo had grown up in the township and had very little knowledge of English, let alone Western culture. But she knew God in such a way that whatever flowed out of her spoke a language of overwhelming love. The space of her one-room, dirt-floor hut was covered by laughing children, drawn to this childlike adult who knew she belonged to a story of compassion and adventure and love larger than her own. And it didn't take long for me to realize that the stuck, frustrated, and bored sides of me were less about my stage of life, or lack of stability, as they were my lost connectivity to those who draw out my dreams and draw me toward passion. Those people like Gogo.

Perhaps you got married or had children, and your life became defined by parenting, providing, or perhaps even surviving, while your passion was put away in the attic. Or maybe it never even made it into your adulthood because it was stored in the rafters of your youth. It is a faded memory, forgotten like teenage love and letter jackets. And we love when passion revisits, but we've trained ourselves not to expect it. At some point maybe we thought we could impact the world, but now, well, we've resigned such childlike thinking.

But what if there was still hope to make an impact on the world? What if that hope narrowed to something as simple as investing in one person?

If every adult got passionate about investing in one person, the world would be changed. Literally. That's not wishful thinking; it's reality. We're passionate about this because we believe that if people like you could unleash your passion for God into the life of one college-aged person, the world would change. Remember, passion is attractive, passion is catalytic, and passion drives us to be a part of something bigger than ourselves—namely, relationships.

Putting Pieces Together

The three of us have had countless conversations with people about spiritual struggles, crushed dreams, broken relationships, and disappointments with God. We're convinced that all of these stem back to three issues: a wonder for God that is lost, an identity that isn't discovered, and a passion that has faded. We all know that other people can be disillusioned by life, but we must also know we're never impervious to that disillusionment ourselves.

Perhaps as you've settled into life, it isn't that wonder, discovery, and passion aren't current realities for you—perhaps they are there—but they're just directed in the wrong places. While these three concepts were created by God, they are capacities that can be filled by all types of substitutes, and they often are. Be honest with yourself: Where might this be the case in your own life? It's only when we recognize these substitutions in our own lives that we can be effective in helping others properly direct theirs.

We've all met men and women, both inside the church and out, who've left their families for someone else, causing everyone to scratch their heads and wonder why they would abandon stability and family in order to risk a moment with someone else. You can probably think of someone by name. We have seen friends dive headfirst into work, chameleonizing themselves to fit the titles their careers have lent, their true identities stripped because of misplaced hope in something in this world. Or perhaps we find ourselves tearing someone down simply to build ourselves up, directing our passions toward our own glory. We assume it's about selfishness, but it's actually passion, pulling us in a direction that is ultimately contrary to the path we truly desire. Our passion is misdirected when we lose the wonder of God and discovering ourselves in light of who He is.

Whether we've realized it or not, our capacity for wonder, discovery, and passion pushes us either forward or backward. How have these three played out in your story? If your life were a book, would these three things only be in previous chapters? If so, we want to encourage you to begin to write them back into your story now. Before we reach into the slow fade happening in a forgotten generation of twentysomethings, we have to acknowledge the slow fade that's happened in our own lives. Wonder, discovery, and passion can no longer be distant childhood memories. They're ongoing, and we'll never fully experience them outside the context of relationships—our relationship with God, our relationship with ourselves (who He made us to be), and our relationships with others.

The same is true for someone of college age. You may have wisdom and experience beyond theirs, but you also have common ground. You are both in search of the same things. You may have discovered some paths deterring healthy wonder, passion, and discovery that they haven't yet, but you're still in process, moving toward the same things.

You need that college-aged person, and that person needs you. Not because you've arrived somewhere they haven't, but because you're both searching for the same things in the same three places— God, yourself, and others.

We take ourselves too seriously. We lose curiosity and imagination. Our God is often too small, possibilities and potential not seen as they used to be—and this is precisely why being relationally connected with a college-aged person has the potential to benefit us as much as it does them. There's a beauty in their idealism, curiosity, and imagination. We believe that connecting your journey of wonder, discovery, and passion with theirs will not only transform them, it will transform you.

Chapter 4

Mentoring Redefined

It would be great if you could be empowered to be a mentor without ever using the word. There is a connotation with it, an empowerment that may not even be realistic. If you wanted to learn how to be a carpenter, you would need a mentor. If you wanted to learn how to be a golfer, you would need a mentor. But all of those denote some sort of completion, a moment where you would be deemed a carpenter or a golfer if you learned the right skills.

In contrast, the spiritual journey of life doesn't have a moment where you get a certificate of completion. Because of that, our jobs as "mentors" feel much different, don't they? The idea of a mentor implies that there is an agenda, that you should have a requirement of what is to be accomplished in the life of the person you are mentoring. If that is true, then when is a person officially "mentored"? When do they arrive at the point of completion? If your goal in being a mentor is to treat a person like a table to be assembled, you will do more damage than good.

Most people we've talked to about investing their lives in college-aged adults don't feel comfortable with the idea. When pressed for a reason, they generally feel the task of mentoring someone is too daunting, that they are underequipped for such an overwhelming responsibility. We believe that is because Christians haven't defined the role of a mentor very well, or possibly because we never defined it and someone drew his or her own unrealistic conclusions.

We can find some comfort in Paul's introductory statement to the Philippians. He says he is "confident of this, that he who began a good work in you will carry it on to completion until the day of Christ Jesus."[7] Paul prefaces his letter of exhortation with the idea that we can do a little bit of good here, but God carries us the distance, not ourselves. As mentors, we have to be careful that we don't develop a messiah complex. We can't start with the self-imposed duty to carry people to a point of completion, a point where we know they will be invincible because they were under our care. If we are honest, that isn't true of us, so why would it be true of them? We know that we ourselves need the grace of God to become who we need to be, and the same is true of every college-aged person. Ultimately, they need *God,* not you. And fortunately, God is the one who bears the responsibility to carry someone to completion, not us. So let's breathe a sigh of relief.

It is an incredible feeling to realize God has entrusted parts of someone's life to you for a season. But we have to remember—He hasn't put us there to take His place. A huge part of mentoring is recognizing what my job is, understanding what God's job is, and making sure I don't get those roles confused.

When mentoring goes wrong, it's usually because somewhere along the way, both the mentor and the mentee have misplaced expectations. If that is true, then what role do you and I play? How do we become non-mentor mentors?

The first and perhaps most critical role of the non-mentor mentor is to begin the process without an agenda. There is a huge difference between treating someone like a person versus treating someone like a project. Projects, not people, require agendas. Each individual represents a story God is telling, and our role is to respect that story and to be careful not to force it into the direction we think it should go.

As we begin the process of mentoring, we should ask, *What is God already doing here?*—not, *What should God begin doing here?* The gift you provide to someone who is a few seasons behind you isn't necessarily what you think it might be. We assume they come to us for answers, but they are often rather looking for a safe place to ask questions. Perhaps you have asked some of the same questions, but just as God is telling a story in your life, you can't force your answers on them.

For example, in a mentor relationship a wide range of topics might be covered. You will talk about God, faith, government, relationships, sex, pain, and hundreds of other topics that come to mind. As an adult, you have probably come to some passionate conclusions in many of these areas. When our roles get confused with God's, we become tempted to direct others toward our own conclusions as they ask questions. In many cases, we make the mistake of defining the mentee's spiritual maturity by his or her ability to see things the way we do. In other words, it's possible to mentor someone who doesn't have the same politics as you. It's possible to mentor someone who thinks about money differently, or even would set different sexual boundaries than you would.

While we can hope for and assume some similarity in beliefs, we have to hold our opinions with open hands. There is a huge difference between one's *beliefs* and one's *opinions*. While these terms can be defined in a variety of ways, Jesus Christ as God's Son is a *belief.* It's something we hold dear, and we are passionate about others believing it too. On the other hand, that Christians should vote for one candidate or another is an *opinion*. We may have a few people we try to share that opinion with, but the mentee can't be on that list. If opinions become the hills we die on, we run the risk of losing a voice in more important areas.

The mentee has a set of experiences, and God has allowed those experiences in his or her life in the same way He has allowed them in yours, whether good or bad. Ultimately, they become more than experiences; they become a lens through which we view the world. Just as your mentee can't have the same experiences you do, he or she can't have identical conclusions about life's toughest questions. God is leading that person on a journey, and the role you play is to help examine past experiences and future hopes and dreams to direct the next steps of that journey. This becomes impossible when an agenda is present and packaged answers are provided.

The second part of becoming a non-mentor mentor is to understand the difference between spiritual maturity and maturing. *Spiritual maturity* is a phrase used as a measuring stick, attempting to quantify how committed someone is to God. To arrive at this standard, we hold the measuring stick up to ourselves; we measure where we are in a few key areas and tell someone else to get to that place. While there are many problems with this, the main one is that we assume the place *we* are is the place God has in mind for someone else. If God is telling a unique story through a set of unique experiences in each individual, how can we ever determine spiritual maturity? In those circumstances, the term *spiritual maturity* seems to be more about the person who says it feeling better about his or her relationship with God than about the person being judged.

In reality, each person comes to faith in Christ from a different starting point. In every relationship, people are either moving closer together or further apart. In other words, every relationship, whether platonic or romantic or familial, is defined by the direction it is moving.

The same is true of one's relationship with God: A person is either moving closer to God or further away. Because a mentee comes to faith in Christ from a different place than you do, the goal is to get that person moving in the right direction and continuing to move in that direction. Depending on past experiences, coming closer to God may happen slowly for some people. At the same time, some start moving closer to God when it seems like they started just a few feet away.

In either situation we celebrate with them as they mature spiritually, not just when they arrive at being spiritually mature. Helping people mature spiritually doesn't have an agenda, while helping people become spiritually mature based on our standards does. When we are helping people mature spiritually, we are helping them discover the next step God is inviting them to take. This may become difficult when there are obvious areas that need changing. In those moments, we have to remember that mentoring is an act of faith, we are trusting God to carry them to completion, and we have respect for the story He might be telling in their lives. Our role is to celebrate the steps they are taking, not highlight the ones they haven't.

Wonder, Discovery, and Passion

As we find ourselves in conversations on a variety of topics and as we check our agendas at the door, wonder, discovery, and passion become an unspoken and organic purpose. As opportunities arise, we seize upon moments to incite wonder, provoke discovery, and fuel passion.

When you start working on a project, arriving at the end is always the mission. When you begin mentoring a person, the process itself is the mission. As the process unfolds, our mission is inciting, provoking, and fueling. As we do that, each of those gives space for the person to discover the path God has for him or her instead of our defining it.

If those three become a framework for us to operate within, whatever topic arises carries with it the potential do one of those three things. Each of these helps clarify our roles:

> We are a catalyst in their stories; we aren't the ones who *tell* their stories.

> We are pushing them toward God; we aren't trying to *be God* for them.

Each of these words gives momentum to the process of God's work in their lives, and they recognize the potential of each individual to have a unique relationship with God. As that relationship forms, God propels the individual into a life of purpose, one not derailed by a measuring stick we created.

Incite

As you begin to think about the story God is telling in your own life, what experiences have incited wonder? What moments have stirred awe for God? Perhaps you can't really define it; you just know there have been moments when you have been overcome with a sense of who God is and what He has done.

As you think about a college-aged mentee, isn't that what you want that person to feel? Isn't that sense of God you had, however long ago, part of the "agenda" you have for the time you spend together? If that person walked away from his or her time with you and had nothing but a sense of awe for who God is, very few of us would feel like we missed the mark.

How do you incite that? While we can't define wonder any more than we can rope the wind, it's easy to know when someone has it and when someone doesn't. Often, we're closest to wonder for God when those around us are chasing it. When people realize they can't understand everything about God and they seem content with the mystery, their sense of awe becomes contagious. Their spark often becomes our spark. As a mentor, being honest about your pursuit of wonder for God can be the thing that incites it in someone else, even if it's not your current reality.

Too often we present God as a problem to be solved, not a mystery to treasure. We get uncomfortable with what we don't know, and we rush to conclusions based on a belief that people with conclusions are more spiritual. Sometimes the deepest wonder can come out of conversations with someone who is relaxing in the mystery of God.

As mentors, we have to wrestle with our language about God, being careful not to draw a picture of God that is finished and concluded, but one that is still being worked out. We have to make sure that our conversations are places where mentees feel free to ask questions about God and to feel as though we are still asking questions too.

To incite wonder, we have to realize the role of the mentor isn't to draw conclusions and answer questions, but to help mentees know that there is a God who loves them, is for them, and died for them, but that much else about God is beyond our capacity to know. The moment we think we know, we realize we don't. We can't predict what He will do, and He isn't a formula we can manipulate to draw the results we want. Our job isn't even handing off our particular picture of who God is. Our job is to incite them on the journey as they develop the picture for themselves.

Provoke

When you think about who you are at your current stage of life, the paths you have taken, the people you have known, the careers you've perhaps had and left, or the girl or guy you could have but didn't marry, what are the common threads of your story? If you had it to do over, would you? Perhaps. But through every part of your story, there are probably incredible lessons learned in the midst of the good and bad that have shaped who you are for good. All of those moments have been critical in helping you discover who you are and perhaps what God is like.

When we begin walking through life with someone, we have to resist the urge to direct that person out of what we perceive to be harm's way every time. Of course there are exceptions, but we have to remember mentoring is about trusting God to tell a story in a person's life, and as He has shaped you through moments of success and regret, He will do the same for your mentee. Your benefit to that person is that you come alongside as someone who has been through many of the same fires, and as the story of his or her life unfolds, you can provoke discussion and questions to help filter through experiences. A win for you is when you have asked the questions that have *led to* conclusions, not when you have *given* conclusions.

Effective mentors may sometimes think the decisions college-aged people make are not good ones, but they don't try to rescue them. These mentors ask questions that help people move out of harm's way. Often at this point in life, college-aged people have an aversion to wisdom unless it comes from within. In not giving answers, these mentors provoke discussions that lead people to their own conclusions, decisions that stick with them. Ultimately, somewhere in those discussions, college-aged people are able to figure out what they believe and think for themselves. They discover truths about themselves and who they are that, had their mentors merely given opinions, may not have happened.

In provoking discovery, we bite our tongues. We resist the urge to fill in the blanks, and we trust that God is going to use broken moments in their lives way beyond our time with them. We trust God is going to use broken moments to help them discover who they are, because after all, that's their story.

Fuel

If you are perfectly honest, you probably don't remember many sermons you heard in your early twenties. Sure, God used them at the time, but years later they are gone. At the same time, we remember every single mission trip, service project, and person we helped find food or shelter. In hindsight, the experiences—not the sermons—fuel our passion for God and our desires to help others. As a mentor, the most teachable moments you have are not going to be in coffeehouses and cafés; they will be when you are participating in experiences together. Perhaps you have somewhere or something you already serve; inviting your mentee into the project with you will perhaps be a lifelong memory and life-altering experience for him or her. While conversations about life are extremely important, opportunities to get outside of our problems and lives and serve the community fuel something inside of us. As a mentor, creating those types of experiences is a gift that can lead a student down a path for life.

We have a lot to give people when we know we are not responsible for their stories—only parts of them. As we release the agenda, define our roles in their lives, and incite, provoke, and fuel, we begin to realize that God uses them in our lives as much as we are used in theirs. We have had countless conversations with mentors who continue to lead others not because they feel they have something to offer but because of what a college-aged individual offers *them*. I hope that's your story. As you take the risk of investing your life into someone else's, God has a way of inciting, provoking, and fueling you, too.

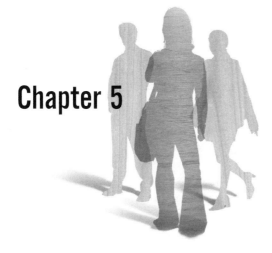

Chapter 5

A New Breed of Leader

Mark is a guy in my (Chuck's) church I've gotten to know pretty well. He's forty-seven years old, married, has two kids, and is almost an empty nester. He has a twenty-four-year-old son, and his daughter is about to graduate from high school and head off to college. He raised his kids in the church and always had some great youth leaders who spent time with his kids, but after high school graduation things changed, and all of a sudden he found himself alone, with no other adults investing in his kids. Now that his daughter is graduating, he's wondering what it will be like for her.

I had a chance to sit down with him one morning, and he began to share his story and concerns with me. This began a great relationship for both him and me. He desperately wanted someone to invest in his kids during their college years. He has a great relationship with each of them, but he told me he can play only so much of a role in their lives. He really wished there were others who would speak into his kids' lives as well. He was a bit discouraged and concerned about who, if anyone, would take the time to invest in his daughter now that she was graduating from high school.

Just being there to listen to him and at times give him insight from my experience was great. But one thing came out of our conversations that I didn't really expect: He wanted to be that outside voice in a college student's life. He has not only seen the need for mentors' voices in the lives of college-aged people, but he felt it as a parent, too. He knew what he would have loved to have, so now he wanted to be that person in the life of another. Through our relationship he now knows he's not alone in this, and I've been able to help him engage with college-aged people in a great way. But he didn't automatically know where to start.

Questions, Concerns, and Hesitations

After dozens of lunches and who-knows-how-many cups of coffee, one day Mark let me know he wanted to begin investing in a college-aged person. But that's all he knew. He had a lot of questions and some real insecurities. He even admitted he was intimidated. None of this surprised me; I know this to be very normal when an older believer starts to think about investing in someone.

He asked, "Where do I start?" and I could tell by the look on his face he was a bit overwhelmed at this whole idea. He shared how he didn't even know what he would say to a guy he sat down with. He wondered if he should go through a book, do a Bible study, or if he should pay for some type of curriculum. He was intimidated by this idea, though, because he doesn't consider himself a "teacher." He even wondered if he had anything to offer a college student. He was filled with insecurities; he didn't know what he was supposed to accomplish or even if there was a direction he was supposed to take someone. To top it all off, he is pretty introverted. He had the heart, but he also had a ton of questions, concerns, and hesitations.

I, on the other hand, didn't have any concerns or hesitations. I love Mark. He has a great heart, is a faithful husband, and is just an all-around great guy. However, the biggest thing for me was simply that he had a heart for college-aged people—and that's all that's needed. From my perspective he just did what most people do—overthink things and make them more complex than they need to be.

So I helped him overcome his intimidation by simplifying a few things.

For Mark, having kids this age began growing his heart for college-aged people. I don't know what circumstances give you that same heart, but I can imagine you have at least some of the same feelings Mark did. Or maybe you've been investing in someone for a while, and you're wondering if you're doing the right things or if you should do something more than you already are. So we're going to walk you through the things I helped Mark understand to help overcome his intimidation. Perhaps this will help you feel more confident with your role in the life of a younger person and even give you a practical direction to take.

The Bigger Picture and Starting Points

Mark had the right heart, and he clearly knew the need, but he had zero direction. This is where I helped simplify some things for him. The first thing I wanted to make sure he understood was that he didn't have to change an entire generation; he just needed to focus on building a relationship with one person. Nothing else is necessary. Once I explained this, I could see a huge weight lift off his shoulders. This clearly made things seem a lot less daunting to him. I wanted him to know that all he needed to do was connect with one person, and if that's all that happened out of this, that was success in my mind. I also let him know there was no time limit and no pressure.

What Mark didn't know was that college-aged people might initially get involved in our churches because we have some sort of weekly college gathering, but they *stay* involved when they're connected to the life of the church. And the life of the church is with people. People like Mark. It's when we can connect college-aged people to the lives of other people that we're successful. It's that simple.

We needed to get Mark connected to someone, and he didn't know where to start. So I asked him if he knew any college-aged guys, he named a few, and we focused on which guy he thought he knew the best—a guy named Shawn.

Maybe you can name one or two college-aged people you know. If so, this is where you should start. If you're coming up blank, ask a youth leader in your church who might know someone you can connect with. It's just a matter of having a starting point. One name.

Shawn just so happened to be attending our church at the time. I encouraged Mark to try to strike up a conversation with him the next Sunday. I told him there was no rush and to just take it one step at a time. Sunday came and went and there wasn't a natural connecting point to start a conversation.

But a couple weeks later he happened to be getting a cup of coffee the same time as Shawn. Mark said hi and asked him how life was going. Shawn shared a little bit, and they went their separate ways. The next week, they ran into each other at the coffeepot again. They began to talk, and after a few minutes Mark said, "Hey, we should grab a cup of coffee sometime during the week and hang out. I'd love to get to know you better." Shawn agreed.

That was it. They were off.

I still remember the day this happened. Mark came up to me after the service and let me know they had set a time for Wednesday afternoon. He looked at me with a ton of excitement … and insecurity. I reminded him that all he had to do was get to know Shawn. Again, no pressure. We connected the next morning to walk through some things I thought might help him stay focused and feel better about their meeting. I wanted to see Mark's insecurity become confidence.

Becoming More Confident

One of the things I always let people like Mark know is that their life experiences are all that's needed. College-aged people need and desire to be connected with people further along in life than they are. And when older believers initiate relationships with them naturally like Mark did, they are typically open to the idea. Especially if it has no agenda, but is just about hanging out for a cup of coffee or a meal. No commitments, just building a relationship.

I wanted Mark to know he could relax. Over time and through a relationship, all he was doing was letting the God-given experiences in his life be used in Shawn's. There was no book needed, no curriculum to teach through, and certainly no other agenda necessary. One thing needed to be accomplished—and that was getting to know each other better. He grew more confident, knowing the lessons he had learned in life may also speak into Shawn's life.

If Mark had gone into this time with a formal agenda, it could have robbed the whole process. The goal we're after is connecting college-aged people to the lives of others. When this happens, we're successful. Going through a book could be useful, but getting them connected to the lives of older believers is the bridge for deeper things. We start with relationships because this is what college-aged people long for.

I wanted to give Mark a sense of direction and potentially prepare him for some things that might pop up during his times with Shawn. I walked him through the following five things.

Ask questions

I told Mark to ask about Shawn's family background, about his direction in life, whether or not he's dating or interested in someone, or what he wants in life. I encouraged him to ask anything that would allow him to get to know Shawn better, and if there was a topic they really clicked with, to just go with it. I reminded him that his job was solely to build a relationship, and building a relationship begins with getting to know each other.

Find commonality

Every relationship has commonalities, and they could be anything. I wanted to make sure Mark knew he was not there to impart information but simply to share experiences with Shawn. Maybe that would happen just over cups of coffee, but maybe he would find out Shawn enjoys baseball, cars, or music as much as he does. I told him it didn't really matter what it was—the point in a mentoring relationship is to find anything to talk about. If it's baseball, figure out a way to go to a game together or invite him over for dinner to watch one. The more we can share life experiences like this with college-aged people, the better. It's totally acceptable if nothing comes up initially. Relationships are built over time, one day at a time. There's no rush, but finding commonality is a great thing to look for.

Be a learner

It's critical we don't feel a need to have all the answers, and we certainly can't view this as a time of imparting information. That's a teacher-pupil relationship, and that's not what we're looking for. If you get asked a question you don't know the answer to, just say you don't know. Maybe you can learn the answer alongside the person who asks. Find a book or other resource on that topic and learn together. Your ability to speak from your life experiences comes in conversation and through a relationship, not through a class or anything formal. Plus, maybe you can learn a thing or two. College-aged people have a ton to offer us as well!

Find a circumstance to capitalize on

There are always points in time when college-aged idealism and life theory don't work out as they thought. It's like those young couples who have all kinds of theories on parenting until they have a child themselves—then theories go out the window and insights from other parents are welcomed. This scenario happens to all of us at one point or another, and these are precisely the times we want to capitalize on. College-aged people have relationships that fall apart, parents who get divorced, loved ones who die, times of confusion with sexuality or belief, and of course a longing for the ever-elusive life direction. These are the times when there is openness to having an outside voice in their lives. I simply encouraged Mark to look for an area where he felt Shawn might be open to having someone speak into his life and slowly begin to speak into that out of his own experiences.

Keep growing

Mark is a guy who really desires to grow in his faith, which is one of the main reasons I was excited for a college-aged guy to be exposed to him. Being involved with someone older like Mark and seeing that person's process is more encouraging to college-aged people than you might realize. If we're continuing to grow we will face struggles, times of confusion, and questions we have a hard time answering.

This entire process is exactly what we want college-aged people to be exposed to. It not only shows them our imperfections in a healthy way, but our process can encourage a college-aged person in their times of confusion and questioning—and they have many. When they see us wrestling to embrace truth in our own lives, they can identify and connect on a deeper level with an older believer in the church. And when they see us simply trying to take one step toward Christlikeness, they are encouraged to do the same. And this is all we're trying to do—take one step ourselves and encourage them in the same direction.

One Step Further

After a few months Mark had gotten to know Shawn pretty well. Shawn had come over a bunch of times for dinner, which is exactly the type of thing we want to see happen. But Mark wanted a little more direction as to where to go from there. He had gotten to know Shawn but wanted to make sure he was doing what was best for him. This was another reason Mark was a perfect candidate to invest in a college-aged person—he had a heart for people. He didn't care about what Shawn might or might not accomplish in life; he just had a heart for him as a human being. This is a perspective we all need to make sure we keep.

The first thing I wanted to do was make sure Mark knew he was already successful in his ministry to Shawn. Shawn was connected to the life of an older believer who genuinely cared for him as a person. This in and of itself is a measurement of success. Shoot, Shawn had even gotten to know where the dishes were in their kitchen. This showed a quality in their relationship that I wish every college-aged person had with an older believer.

I did, however, encourage Mark to take this is a step further. A beautiful thing about this relationship was that Shawn was not only connected to an older man but also to a family. This is priceless. Shawn hears their thoughts about and hearts for their own kids, he gets insights into their marriage, and he is even exposed to some of the dysfunction in it. This is great for a guy like Shawn because, like more than half of all college-aged people, he grew up in a broken home with no marriage to look to as a model.

But Mark could take this a step further and help Shawn connect to the body of Christ in an even deeper way. Mark and his wife also know other types of people in our church. People like Mark's family are connected to others in the church who are perfect for investing in younger people. Mark and his wife know single moms and dads, elderly widows, and young married couples. Now that he was connected to Shawn, I encouraged him to help Shawn connect with his other friends. I encouraged him in some practical ways like having the elderly widow over for dinner the same night as Shawn. I also threw out the idea of thinking through an area of Shawn's life that maybe another friend could speak to. If there was something Shawn was wrestling with that one of his friends had already dealt with, he could easily connect them.

Because Mark earned Shawn's trust through a relationship, he could now capitalize on this and help Shawn connect to the life of our church in an even deeper way. It's important to realize that college-aged people want to be connected relationally in these ways.

People like Shawn might come around to a church service or two or possibly attend a college gathering, but if they're not connected relationally to the life of the church, they inevitably detach and the slow fade continues.

I want to encourage you to simply initiate something with someone. Just one person. Take it slowly, and over time seek to build a relationship. Maybe it begins with hanging out by the coffeepot or doughnut table. Maybe you already know someone you can be more intentional with. Or maybe you simply begin by letting a youth leader know you're open to investing into a college-aged person.

I don't think it matters who is teaching on Sunday mornings at your church. I don't even think it matters what kind of music you have. I've seen college-aged people stay in churches simply because they're invited by and sitting next to the older believer who is investing in them … someone just like you.

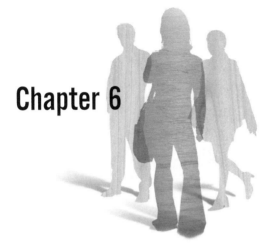

Chapter 6

Community of Faith

It took me (Abbie) about a week in the following-Jesus journey to realize college students lacked a voice in the church. It was a Saturday morning in the spring of my freshman year. I was tired of studying and far more interested in this new faith I'd come upon, so I decided to visit the local bookstore. Not only did I discover thousands of books offering a range of Christian voices, but I discovered no books offering the voice of a Christian in college. When someone informed me that there was such a thing as a "Christian bookstore," I breathed a sigh of relief, assuming such a niche must shelve college-aged perspectives. But I left there deflated too.

My naive eighteen years pondered, "This isn't possible. College-aged people are the culture changers. We're the ones who drive the film, fashion, technology, and entertainment industries. We're the radicals who can shift an election! We're the natural revolutionaries! So of all places, it seems like the church would be the one sanctioning college-aged people, tapping into their views and energy."

The lesser story here is that I decided to compile a book by college students about faith. The larger story, however, was a realization that the voice of college students was silent in modern church.

In most communities of faith, the role of the college-aged person is benchwarming at best—but more commonly, disconnected altogether. Without this voice, we're not only neglecting valuable souls in our midst, but we're also diminishing the grander story of our whole.

Widow of the Twenty-First Century

There's a story in Acts 6 that's terribly similar to our story today. In verses 1–7, a sector of the community is recognized as neglected.[8] Though the church was growing numerically, widows were being overlooked in daily distributions. Not only did this threaten a destruction of church unity, but it distracted from the larger vision.[9] Leaders of that era stopped what they were doing, reevaluated the current situation, and sought to resolve it accordingly. Widows, they realized, must be reprioritized into the communal tapestry. Displaying great humility and intentionality, then, they restructured their current approach.

What if college-aged people are the widows of a twenty-first-century church?

In Acts 6, the whole community took ownership for the disparity, and unity was restored. They became aware of a need, evaluated the need, and then reorganized their approach in order to meet the need. Maybe it's time that we do the same. Maybe it's time we listen to our widows' needs, take ownership of our disparities, and move toward resolution.

Starting Line

There's a child in every college-aged person, and there's an adult in them as well. The job of a mentor is to nullify neither and cultivate both, leveraging their youth while leading them into adulthood. Too often, adults neglect both because neither is categorically complete (youth or adult). Young Christ-followers are trained to believe a message of salvation as the ticket to a life of ease and answers. But then tragedy (or reality) hits, and they find they have no framework for understanding life, let alone an apparently good God, in such contexts. The follower is too much of an adult to go crying to mommy and daddy, but not adult enough to process such pain. They're in between, in transition, and in need of knowing they're not alone—in need of knowing that God and a community of God-followers are *with them* and working toward an end of good.

College-aged people don't need answers as much as they need guidance and a safe community in which they'll find space to grow. The goal of a personal investment in them isn't a "mini me" or an ideal picture of adulthood. The goals of investment are realigned expectations and awakened states of belonging. When expectations move from their immediate families or the world around them and are transferred to connectivity, belonging in the faith, and the hope and love of a God beyond them, the mentor has done well. When the heritage of family moves beyond the one they grew up in and the impact of their life is realized as eternally transformative, the slow fade begins to abate. When college-aged people know they belong to God and play a crucial role in God's story through a church, the personal investment is a success.

More so than searching for a marked finish line, then, the goal of a mentor is to remain in forward motion toward renewed starting lines, toward restored voices and visibility to that which has been invisible—toward God.

No one finds belonging by being told a list of rules or being taught a three-point sermon—we find belonging by being connected to a role and a range of relationships. We mature spiritually not by learning how to be superhuman, but by learning how to lean into our need for God and others when we bump up against life and our own humanity.

To know that we belong to God and are part of God's community of faith gives us a sturdy hope to stand on and a satisfying reason to embark upon the wonder, passion, and discovery we were made for. When the college-aged person is plugged into the community of faith, all sides of the equation are transformed. *If you show me my role, I will show up. If you show me my place of belonging, I will come.*

Not everyone is called to do everything, but everyone is called to do something. Translation: College-aged people have a role. They belong to God's story. And as mentors, we have the chance to help awaken that. They're not fading from our faith communities because they want to; they're fading because they don't know where they belong. They've never been connected to a community of belonging. They've never been shown another way.

But what exactly is "another way"?

We mean the kind of community where everyone has a name, and where people notice if you don't show up.

We mean reaching out *to them*. Friend them on Facebook, follow them on Twitter, or call them with no other agenda than asking how they are. You'd be surprised how rarely such reaching out happens and how meaningful it is when it does.

We mean valuing people whether single, married, or any other status. Being willing to love them, especially when they've messed up, whether by getting drunk, hooking up, getting caught cheating, or falling into any other transgression. Connecting them to a community of faith means teaching them they can never outrun the reach of grace.

We mean treating them as if they're really going to lead the next generation and the next generation's church.

Connectivity

Modeling after our relational God (three-in-one), we are relational beings whose spiritual, intellectual, and relational growth is contingent upon cooperation with the Holy Spirit and surrounding body. When you invest in one life, you're inviting one life into *many*. You're expanding a paradigm from snapshot to story—from an expectation and determined endpoint where they will be X, Y, or Z to a lifelong journey of becoming who God is making that person to be, and belonging to the identity and community God has provided.

Being connected means knowing where I belong. So, we can't keep trying to fit spiritual maturity in a box. We can't expect candy-fed faiths based on emotion and reaction to end at anything beyond disappointment. And we can't expect saying a prayer, tithing a percentage, or reciting a certain passage to construct a lasting connection. We must invite them into a different story.

Connecting college-aged people with their roles in the church means inviting their involvement in the church's redemptive story. Halting the slow fade means validating any life-stage as crucial to the life of the church at large and inviting all lives into relationship with the day-to-day life of the church and the church's people.

When I reflect on my faith process, relational connectivity and opportunities to serve have been pivotal in my spiritual maturity. My first interaction with the faith community entailed about forty college students gathering every Thursday on the third floor of the science building. I thought this was incredible. But what was more incredible was that I got to be connected to it. And then I got invited to a large church, where I realized Christianity wasn't just a passionate phase of forty friends on Thursday night, but it was a paramount story being lived out by thousands. Again, I thought this was incredible. And I got to be connected to it. And then I got invited on an overseas mission trip. And as I sat at a teahouse in China listening to college students tell me "how benevolent" our God was, I realized this paramount story of God's love was a profound story for the world. And I got to be connected to it.

Experiences devoid of relational connections cease to cause transformation. The following certainly isn't an exhaustive list, but it should at least lend some ideas to your role in helping leverage connectivity and belonging for this age-stage:

- College-aged people are passionate about getting their hands dirty. They love diving into issues and ideologies, marching for causes, and feeling like an active participant in making the world a better place. So let them dig.

- If they're artists or musicians, encourage the importance of their work and voice in the church.

- Wrestle with them through theological topics, exploring different viewpoints and theologians throughout the ages, like Karl Barth on singleness, Augustine on education, or Mother Teresa on service.

- Help bridge them into roles of service. As Martin Luther King Jr. said, "Everyone can be great, because everyone can serve."

- Invite a college-aged person to serve with you this month, or if they're already invested in a cause, ask if you can tag along.

- Be creative with them, expanding their horizons of "service"—challenge them to care for someone for less than five dollars by visiting inmates, a local shelter, or an orphanage; sharing a meal with a homeless person; or taking a meal to someone who's sick.

Kindness, not rules or coercion, leads to repentance. You're not loving them or serving for the sake of an agenda or producing something. You're doing so for the sake of moving a step further into God's story.

Family Meeting

"Family meetings" were my non-churchgoing family's "church," I guess. We'd discuss important issues families must discuss, like who's on dish duty this week or the date of the next family outing to the bowling alley. As a kid, family meetings were great. But then my sister and I hit the teen years and "great" hit the fan. Conversations turned more serious, to topics like allowance or getting grounded for skinny-dipping in the neighborhood lake. Interrupting each other and too many tearful conclusions of slammed doors caused my parents to establish the "spoon rule."

Only the person holding the spoon was allowed to talk. And when that person was finished talking, he or she would pass the spoon to the next candidate. And for whatever reason, it worked brilliantly. The spoon was like a magic microphone that gave the speaking person the dignified role of speaking, and other people the clarified role of listening. It didn't raise my allowance or stop me from skinny-dipping, but it taught us to listen to one another again.

As a faith community, we've got to find a spoon. We've got to find a way to reorganize our table so that no voice is being overlooked, let alone fading out altogether. Each part is necessary for our whole. All lives are powerful agents toward transforming every life to come.

Revolution happens when ideas or practices take a radical shift and as leaders have the chance to be catalysts for both. A healthy church means a healthy body of people learning to follow Jesus, and a healthy body of people means everyone knows his or her role. No one else in all of history or the future can do what any one individual was made to do and be and become. Every story is unique and every story pertinent to our whole. When tethered properly, college-aged people may be our most transformative agents in bringing God's love to the world. They are searching for an invitation into life's grander story—a window of belonging in a story bigger than their own—and mentors have the chance to send that invitation. So either they continue to fade away from faith—meanwhile trying to change the world—or mentors show them their places of belonging, and we watch the world change together.

Telling God's Story

If you need a grand finale, we aren't your people. Our fireworks show is about thirteen words long: *Halting the slow fade happens when adults start investing in college-aged people.* Engaging their hearts and minds doesn't require anything fancy; it requires a willingness toward mutual fascination with one another and an openness toward sharing a journey together.

Our temptation will always be to hurry up and find a solution, but God will never be in a hurry, nor does He need our solutions. He knows the state of the slow fade, and He isn't overwhelmed. But He's also authored us to a point where we've recognized an invisible entity of our whole, and it's time to shift gears. It's time for a new chapter.

Building a sturdy faith takes an intergenerational community. Spiritual maturity validates every part as crucial to the whole. We need one another. By choosing to invest in the college-aged person, you're choosing to invest in the future. You're choosing to invest in *every* generation. You're choosing to bring hope and ultimate transformation to every corner of the world.

Our stories are designed to be part of a bigger one, and the story between you and a college-aged person folds into a story being written by the church, a story of compassion and healing, of inclusion and restoration. Faith is a process and cannot relandscape decades in a span of months or remodel habits through the confines of an agenda.

We're invited to play a role in God's story, to join Him in awakening a dying world to redemption and reconciliation, to share in mutual fascination with a resurrected Savior. These college-aged people are part of this bigger story. So are you. Together, we have the chance to demonstrate that story to the world.

Chapter 7

Mutual Transformation

I (Reggie) started taking pictures when I was in the ninth grade. My football coach cut me from the team and handed me a camera. Since then I have considered myself an amateur photographer, and it has been a great outlet for me. I wish I could convince you that my love for photography is linked to worship, but my wife would accuse me of using that as an excuse to buy more gear and blame God for the bill.

I have always been fascinated with the world around me. Anything that has God's stamp on it amazes me. When I use a macro lens to catch a dragonfly, a telephoto to shoot a humming-bird, or a wide-angle to catch a cloud configuration at sunrise, I experience something that is hard to explain. I am in awe. Trust me. It has nothing to do with my ability to capture an image; it is the power of seeing God's handiwork, up close, in all its brilliance. The great photographers of the world have a certain kind of fascination with their subjects. They see things in ways ordinary people don't see them because they have an obsession with finding the magic in everything. They capture an angle or a moment that makes people stop and see something extraordinary that they may have never noticed otherwise. Objects most of us would pass by every day, objects that are invisible to us, can take on new life when seen through the eyes of a skilled photographer.

It can be ordinary things:

a road

a tree

a cloud

a shoe

a child

It is not the subject alone that fascinates the photographer. It is something else.

Sure, every photographer is trying to get the right picture.

Photojournalists try to seize a defining moment.

Wedding photographers try to capture the passion.

Nature photographers try to record a miracle of creation.

Portrait photographers try to find a timeless expression.

But talented photographers see something that makes the difference in a superior image. Skilled photographers are fascinated by light. They study it. They measure it. They analyze it. They understand its temperature. They manipulate their position until they have captured the right amount of ambience.

They know that light is everything. A gifted photographer is fascinated by the power of light to transform his subject into something amazing.

As strange as it may seem, I am fascinated by the light I see reflected in the souls of people around me. Over the past decades of my life, I have been amazed at the transformation I have seen in so many ordinary people because of God's light in their lives. During my younger years I think I passed by a lot of people the same way I would pass everyday objects, rarely noticing their potential. I seldom recognized the light of God's image at work in their lives.

Something has happened to me over the past decades that's hard to explain. Maybe it's just part of growing older. I have a new fascination with people, regardless of their beliefs, stages of life, backgrounds, or races. I have a curiosity that I believe is God-driven. I have started making an assumption that everyone I meet, whether they realize it or not, is connected to a divine story. So I am naturally curious when I am involved with people, looking for the angle where God's light is reflected in their lives. Sometimes the light is extremely obvious, other times it is dim, but it is almost always there. Even in those who don't know God, there is a spark of His image. It's the reason most people are so quick to embrace a friend, aid in a crisis, and love their families.

We could debate this theologically, but I'm convinced that even though the human heart is drawn to selfishness and sin, we were still created in God's image. Sure the image has been blurred, and our nature tends to stray toward darkness, but there is still something fascinating about anyone whom God has created. Somewhere along my journey, I grew to the place where I realized I needed to be more involved in the personal lives of people. I can't tell you exactly how and when you should invest in someone's life. I don't even know how to decide whom you should choose as a friend. I just know that for me it's like taking the right picture. When someone catches your attention and the light is just right, you see it, and you sense that this is a unique moment. Your life begins to change when you understand, in a small way, how God sees those around you.

Here's the important part: You are not getting involved with others because they need you to help them, or even because they are amazing people. You are stepping into their lives because you are compelled by something bigger than you and them. You are making a choice to participate in something that God has been doing since time began in a garden. You are choosing to engage in a story that has transcended every generation and is continuing to impact the people around you. It is a story of redemption and restoration. Don't miss it, and don't make the mistake of thinking that your purpose is simply to be used by God to help someone change. More than likely, a lot of things still need to be restored in your life as well. It was a critical discovery for me when I realized I was not the answer for everyone else's life, but that my relationship with others was intended to have a transforming effect on *my* life as well.

I heard Chris Wiersma, a young pastor in Canada, recently say that mutual fascination results in mutual transformation. Nothing can transform my soul like the handiwork of God. And when I approach any relationship with a healthy fascination of what God is doing in someone's life, and that person does the same with me, it has the potential to transform us both.

I don't really know how to explain it, but many of my transforming moments in the past twenty years have happened because of involvement with those who are teenagers and college-aged.

Jared showed up at our church as a senior in high school after his parents divorced. He had been somewhat betrayed by the Christian leaders in his life, but he still managed to become active in our student ministry. After college, he attended Fuller Theological Seminary, and he came home every month to help us design curricula for teenagers. His skeptical and analytical approach to faith has transformed him into a thoughtful communicator to students. Countless conversations with Jared through the years have inspired me to keep looking at the next generation through a unique lens.

Jared is transforming the way I view culture.

Ashley became a friend of my family's when she was nineteen, after she had moved to Atlanta from Canada. She grew up in a legalistic, fringe religious group that abused the concept of God in her life. Although she has a kind and considerate personality, she is not interested in any kind of religious system that sees her as a project or someone to fix. One day she blindsided me with a question that made me take a hard look at my Christian motives as a leader: "If I never become a Christian, will you still be my friend?"

Ashley is transforming the way I value relationships.

Andrew traveled with me to shoot video of our Orange Tour. He has a sarcastic, dry sense of humor that he sometimes uses to cover up a genuine sincerity for being part of God's work. Although Andrew is not in college, he is an avid learner and worker. He is intentional about spending blocks of time with adults who are older, and he pursues opportunities to contribute to any team trying to create something relevant. I have personally learned to value the creative input and insight I get from this twenty-year-old.

Andrew is transforming the way I define relevance.

Jen works in a restaurant where I eat several times each week. The first time she described her spiritual journey, I was intrigued with her authenticity and honesty. Although she was not sure she was a Christian, she was more excited about figuring out who God is than most church people I know.

Jen is changing the way I pursue God.

Alex works in our IT department. He spends most of his day fixing the parts of our world we can't live without. His personality can be intimidating because he knows so much about things I will never understand. Most of the conversations I have with him during the week I could not possibly remember, but I have had conversations with him about his dad that I will never forget. His determination to become the right kind of man is inspiring.

Alex is transforming the way I understand family.

There are host of people in their early twenties who influence me.

Every summer I spend a couple of months with college interns at BigStuf camps in Panama City. I was invited several years ago to train and lead them, but most summers they teach me. Some of my favorite memories of camp are hanging out with them at lunch, at Waffle House, or on a hotel balcony late at night discussing a variety of issues. I have been doing it for almost a decade, and now some are married, having children, and heading into their thirties. Some have become close friends, and many of them have encouraged, inspired, and challenged me in ways they will never know.

I never wonder where these individuals would be now if I hadn't been in their lives. Instead, I wonder where I would be if they hadn't been in mine.

I hope I have influenced them in some positive ways. I have watched them switch majors in college, deal with divorced parents, struggle with faith issues, date, get engaged, break off engagements. I have officiated their weddings, baptized them, talked them through career choices and ministry decisions, watched them get involved in mission causes, and seen them take leadership roles in churches. In most of their situations, other adults besides me were heavily invested in their lives; in some cases I was the only one. But don't miss the point: What happened in me was just as important as what happened in them. I have simply decided that I want to learn to see the potential light in whomever I meet, especially those who are college-aged. I don't want to miss the extraordinary potential that is *them*. I want to continue to be fascinated by what God is writing into their lives, wherever they may be on the spectrum of faith. It's not just that I want to keep their faith from fading; I want to keep mine from fading as well.

We all need horizontal, or peer-to-peer, relationships. Friendships matching our stages of life give us a level of acceptance, accountability, and care that other relationships can't give us. I need friends who are married, who can recognize Don Henley's voice, and who are stressed about affording college for their kids—just like me. Likewise, there is a need for those who are college-aged to connect with peers so they can build networks, make their personal marks, and find identity with their own tribes.

But it's also critical to have intergenerational, or vertical, relationships. They can take us a little deeper and challenge us in positive ways. Those of us who are older adults should strive to be intentional about pursuing healthy relationships with those in our businesses and churches who are college-aged. I am in a fortunate stage of life where I don't have to work at investing in those who are eighteen to twenty-five years of age. All I have to do is invite my kids to dinner or do something on a weekend, and it's an automatic intergenerational gathering. It is not unusual for any dinner or weekend event to involve a host of college-aged people. But when this stage is over, I must still make those who are college-aged a priority.

If you want to continue to be transformed as an adult, you need to be intentional about pursuing relationships with those who are college-aged. The best way to protect your own spiritual passion from fading may be to make sure you're investing in the lives of the people around you. It seems like a basic principle we should all have realized as adults, but what I'm suggesting is that if you want to stretch your faith, if you are hungry to breathe new life into the spiritual dimension of your life, consider spending time investing in a teenager and helping carry that person into his or her college years. You will be transformed.

Appendix A

A Note to Ministry Leaders

In the fall of 1999, I (Chuck) was hired to start a college ministry at Cornerstone Church in Simi Valley, California. I was excited about the church and especially the opportunity to start a ministry from scratch. At the time, the church had about eight or nine hundred people in attendance, but there was nothing specifically for college-aged people. In fact, the only "database" they had was a blue Post-it note with six people's names written on it, people who were supposedly interested in a college ministry. I would have contacted all six, but only four had phone numbers listed. Simi Valley is a far cry from a college town, but there is a community college the next city over. So I set off, looking to start something that had an impact on the people in the area—whoever they were.

I started things off with a barbecue for anyone college-aged. Nine people showed up besides the youth pastor and myself. It was a great time hanging out and getting to know one another, and from there we started a weekly gathering. We met in a stale classroom with no sound system (the running joke was that orphanages in third-world countries had more atmosphere than that room). When we did have someone to lead worship, we projected songs on a white wall with an overhead transparency. It was simple—no "bells and whistles"—but the ministry began to grow.

We moved from one room to the next as more people kept coming, and it was an exhilarating time as people began to connect with others in their life-stage. We went one day at a time, and before we knew it, we were three years down the road with a staff of interns and more than nine hundred college-aged people coming every week. It was everything I had hoped for.

That is, until I stepped back and took a hard look at things.

Although I loved Cornerstone and those I worked with, the truth was I viewed the church as a means for me to build my ministry. To put it bluntly, I was building an empire using the church's finances and resources. I would never have worded it that way, and I'm fairly certain nobody else would've either, but that's the truth. I had created little more than a parachurch organization that just happened to be under the umbrella of a local church. We had a different mission statement, and we had no strategy for creating sustainable connecting points between college-aged people and the rest of the church. Well, let me rephrase—when it came to budget and resources, I made sure there was a sustainable connection. As you can probably tell, I'm not proud of that.

Our ministry looked great from the outside, and people from other churches were calling me for advice, but I began asking myself what all this was ultimately accomplishing. It was a confusing time for me because I had always viewed this type of ministry as a measurement for success, but as I began questioning it, I started to rethink everything.

Deconstruction and Healthy Processes

I began to wonder—if we stopped our weekly gathering, what would happen to all these people? Most of them would probably disappear. This is when I was hit with the hard reality that what we had created was not sustainable. It was a tough thing to face, but I wanted to do what was best for the college-aged people I had grown to love. And if they began to disappear, they were never really connected in the first place. In my head first, then in practice, I began a healthy process of deconstructing everything we had built.

The first thing I changed was how I referred to our ministry. I used to call it a "university ministry," but I began referring to it as a "ministry to college-aged people." This might seem like semantics, but for me it was huge. In my mind, this put the focus solely onto the people as individuals, and this subtle tweak of wording began to change everything. If this was a ministry to individual human beings and I had a responsibility in their lives as a pastor and shepherd, I had to make sure we were doing what was best for them. And I was convinced we had to change some things in order to make that happen.

I always knew that God was interested in bringing people toward the likeness of Christ one step at a time.[10] My philosophy of ministry, however, wasn't designed to help in this process—it was all about a large gathering. Yes, we had small groups and they were beneficial, but if the large-group gathering had died, so would these groups. And again, the instability of our ministry strategy hit me. I had to change the focus from getting college-aged people connected to our gatherings to making sure they were connecting intimately to other people. In fact, Paul tells us in Ephesians 4:11–14 that God uses His gifted people to bring us toward maturity. This is why connecting people to each other is so important. If not, their maturity process is going to be robbed.

I ended up taking this a step further because of Paul's command to older men in 2 Timothy 2:2 and to women in Titus 2. In these passages, Paul commands the older believers to invest in younger people. People to people. So, not only were gifts used, but the life experience of the older believer was too. I began thinking through how we could help college-aged people connect to people of different generations as my definition of success (as well as my ministry strategy) was beginning to reshape.

I realized something else: College-aged people desire to be connected in deeper ways to the church as a whole. They want to know they belong in the church—not just one ministry—but they don't know how. As I thought about this, our ministry's role in these people's lives became clear. Our ministry was now about helping college-aged people move toward relational connection with older believers, beyond a program or service. It wasn't that we had to forgo our weekly program—it wasn't an either-or issue—it was a matter of recognizing what was sustainable and concentrating on that. Relationships aren't just what college-aged people want; it's actually the only sustainable connecting point we can offer them.

Necessary Steps

I eventually concluded that if I was going to make sure college-aged people were connected to the lives of older adults, we had to focus *everything* we did on this. This is when I changed both my job description and my definition of success. Our ministry was no longer about getting people to come to programs; it was about getting them intimately connected to other people—and specifically to older believers.[11] I had figured out how to get people to come to a weekly gathering and winter retreats, but I had to experiment with practicalities to implement this new direction.

Over the last eight years I have homed in on five things as I sought to implement this new strategy, and I've found this strategy to be much simpler and more sustainable than I originally thought. This is applicable to any strategy you may already have, whether that's small groups, a large gathering, or nothing at all. It all comes down to some basic characteristics that need to be adapted in everything we do. I've been a part of implementing these in a very large church, and I have carried these over into the church I planted, Colossae Church. I believe they are necessary for connecting college-aged people to the life of our church, and they're applicable in any church.

Define success by relational connection

Changing our definition of success on paper doesn't help; we actually have to embrace it. The extent to which we help college-aged people connect relationally with older people in our church, and specifically older believers, is the extent to which we consider ourselves successful. (For more on how we go about that process, refer back to chapter 5.)

The other day I got an email that displayed the connectedness a college-aged person has with older believers in our church. Kelsey put together a "date night out" for couples, and she and her friends watched the kids while the parents went out to dinner. This was encouraging to me in itself, but it's the reason she gave for wanting to do this that got me even more excited. She said she noticed some parents never had the chance to just get away by themselves. She talked about the tiredness she saw in them and even mentioned some of her conversations about this with a few parents. The fact that she saw a need shows her connection, not only with one person but with multiple families. This was a huge sign of success for us, and one of the types of things we use to measure our success.

It's one thing to have college-aged people serve in our churches. But for me it's an entirely different thing when a college-aged person wants to start a ministry because she sees a need in older believers. They served Kelsey by investing in her, and now she wants to serve them. Another budget line or program isn't necessary to be effective; we just need to be very intentional about connecting people to people. Defining success relationally and focusing on it is at the core of effectiveness.

That all sounds great, right? But there are some implications to this definition, and the first one is getting older believers to understand what we're doing.

Help older believers embrace their responsibility

When we don't intentionally connect college-aged people with people outside a college ministry, our lack of action only contributes to the separation of generations. A lot of leaders find this same chasm in their churches. This is precisely why having a strategy beyond a program or gathering point is so important, regardless of what we may already have in place. It all begins with helping older believers embrace the commands in 2 Timothy and Titus 2.

This is why my job description needed to change—now, I had to include helping older believers follow through with this command.

As the pastor of a church, I now gauge whether or not we're effective by how many older believers are following through with the command to invest in younger people. It's one thing to be concerned about the disconnection, but I need to make sure I'm doing my part in holding older believers accountable to these commands. If older believers aren't being faithful in this, I take that as a negative reflection on my leadership and an indication of my ineffectiveness to model this for my church.

This should start from us as leaders. Even if that's not the mentality of the person leading your church, it can still start with you! It's just a matter of starting with one relationship. It's important to remember what we're suggesting will work alongside any strategy you might already have—we're simply connecting people to people.

Invest in families

Holistically investing in families is another characteristic that helps bridge relational connections. By partnering with an entire family—versus just the parents or one child in a particular age-stage—we can bridge intergenerational connections naturally. Families are made up of different generations, personalities, and gift sets. So the partnership of church and family is crucial to creating a natural bridge for college-aged people.[12] You don't need to spend much time with college-aged people to see their interest in marriage. Initially they might be a bit shy to ask questions about your marriage, but give them enough time and that will change. With over half of college-aged people growing up in single-parent homes, families are very intriguing.

I have guys ask me questions all the time about my marriage, and girls are constantly asking my wife questions. I've had countless college-aged people tell me how much they enjoy spending time getting to know couples in our church. When they get to know them, they not only feel like part of their families, they watch and learn from them. And even when they see dysfunction in marriages, it's healthy. Countless couples get married and have no clue how hard things can actually be. Parents can often hide these struggles from their own kids, but being connected to other couples outside of their parents can help them catch the reality of marriage. They inherently know things can't always be perfect, so seeing struggle *and* perseverance in a marriage is often encouraging for them.

Just ask a college-aged person if he or she would be interested in hearing from couples about how their relationships work. If you get one negative response, let me know personally, because it would be a first.

Value difference in a healthy way

Ephesians 4:11–12 teaches us the necessity of being around people who are gifted differently, and Paul's commands in Titus 2 show us the necessity of being connected to those of different generations.

To protect this value and to avoid creating chasms between generations, we need to help people understand the beauty of being in relationships with others who are different from them and to be careful about only being in relationships with people just like them.

Moving in this direction may initially be tough for some people, especially those who have been around church for a while, because they are typically used to pursuing only people like themselves. I've had some older believers tell me that being around these younger believers made them feel old and that they wanted to be able to connect with other people in their stage of life. There is certainly value in connecting people in this way, but we also have to protect and preserve a value of difference—even if it means having some tense conversations. I had to keep encouraging them to live out and embrace Paul's commands, forcing them to think through why they never did this. I had to remind them that they were responsible for younger people in our church and that this was a biblical mandate, not our own. I also gently but firmly confronted some people on their consumer mentality and asked them to seriously consider where their hearts were on the issue.

It's funny because, over time, these same people became the ones who are now helping preserve this value in our church. They appreciate it because they see how college-aged people can speak into their lives, and they see the beauty of investing in someone younger. I encourage the older believers to recognize this as a blessing for their obedience. Once you get people moving in this direction, they'll never turn back.

Placing a high value on difference in this way keeps all types of people connected, including college-aged people. They don't get pushed aside by older believers, but rather they are intentionally pursued by and connected to them. This characteristic creates a sense of oneness that's extremely attractive to college-aged people because they naturally explore different things in life, particularly things that are different from what they grew up with. So to be connected to a group of people who are all different from one another and yet unified is exactly what they want. And perhaps most importantly, this value allows college-aged people to be an active part of that unified group. This is another reason why relational connection is sustainable.

The important thing is to slowly begin talking about this characteristic with people. And remember, this begins simply by you personally embracing this value. You model it. You share it. You help older believers embrace it, and when they do, you expose college-aged people to them. It's that simple.

Allow college-aged people to have a voice

College-aged people want to be part of solutions. This is one reason they're so involved in things like social justice projects—they see an issue and can have a role in solving it. Every church is thinking through issues, trying to solve problems, and it's the churches that value the voices of college-aged people in those conversations that are attractive.

Reggie, Abbie, and I are constantly asking the opinions of college-aged people. We might ask people in our churches or at a coffee shop, but we have conversations because we see value in these people. I am often shocked at their insights, and it's easy for me to assume things that aren't actually true about them if all I do is talk about them with other leaders. As leaders we can read books about statistics of college-aged people dropping out of churches, but we need to be careful about making this a scientific research project. We need to start by simply asking the opinions of those in our churches. We need to include them, value them, and give them a role in being part of a solution.

Granted, some ideas and thoughts they give can be extremely idealistic, but that's part of the beauty too. If necessary we can help them think through things more practically, but their idealism is often good for us. We can easily lose that idealism in our own lives, and this is part of the value their voices bring to our churches.

Perhaps the most important thing I need to say here is that we have to *listen* to what they are saying. They will know if their voices aren't being heard. If you ask and don't listen, it's not worth it. They need to know their opinions and thoughts are taken to heart. We don't always have to agree or follow them to the letter; we just need to make sure we take them seriously. When college-aged people are included in solutions for the church as a whole, they desire to stay connected. Being a part of a college-aged gathering point might be the initial door they walk through into our churches, but having a voice and being connected to those in the church is why they stay.

Appendix B

Myths and Hesitations

You may be in a position where you desire your church to embrace ministry to college-aged people, but some leaders in your church may be more hesitant or possibly totally opposed. Whenever we have conversations with staff or leaders about developing a more effective plan for those who are college-aged in the church, there are a host of responses. We want to help by preparing you for some of the responses or push-backs you might get to these myths. Here, we want to discuss nine responses typically heard in opposition and then give our brief responses to them.

Isn't that what campus ministries do?

Campus ministries are usually good at establishing peer-to-peer relationships, not intergenerational relationships. What's more, not every college-aged person attends a college campus or has access to these ministries.

There is not enough budget.

Budget is usually not an issue if your priority is a relationally driven model.

This is not a college town or community.

More than likely, college-aged people are still close by. Again, many of the people of this age are not in college; in fact, only an estimated 25 percent of eighteen- to twenty-five-year-olds attends a four-year college full time.

We don't know how to appeal to college students.

Those who are college-aged have a basic need for the kinds of leaders who will create an environment where they can belong. It's simply a matter of embracing the simplicity of what we talk about in this book—one-on-one relationships.

We've tried doing it before, and it doesn't work.

Maybe you tried a programmed college-student ministry instead of recruiting leaders who minister on an individual basis to those who are college-aged. Consider trying a different approach.

This is not a long-term investment; they will leave our church when they graduate.

You are actually protecting your investment and the investment other churches have made through children's and youth ministries. Consider it from a different perspective: Missionaries aren't necessarily part of the local church, either, but we see them as valuable investments.

We can't hire another staff person.

That's okay, but you can still mobilize adults who will invest their time in those who are college-aged.

It's hard to see how this would benefit our church.

Then you may not see how this age group can be a catalyst to keep you more relevant, serve in critical roles as volunteers, and ultimately become leaders who will redefine the church as a viable influence in culture. The fact that you don't see the value shows you haven't invested enough time in college-aged people.

These are the years they should solidify their faith on their own.

Do you really think people should solidify their faith alone? It's one thing to have space to process your own faith, but that doesn't mean you should be disconnected from a community of faith where there is a sense of belonging, especially at a time when you are making the most critical decisions of your life.

Appendix C

Shifting Perspectives

It can be tough interacting with an age-stage entirely removed from your own. And as much as the following doesn't mean to be prescriptive, we hope it lends some fresh ideas. During hundreds of conversations with college-aged people, we have found the "Instead Ofs" to be a standard approach in relating to them ... and would like to propose the "How Abouts" as an alternative.

INSTEAD OF:

"How is someone like you not dating or married?"

HOW ABOUT:

"It's really good to see you." (In other words, validate God's movement, regardless of their marital status. Confirm their value *just as they are*.)

INSTEAD OF:

"Don't worry—when you stop looking, Mrs./Mr. Right will come along,"

HOW ABOUT:

"It sounds like where you are could be a tough place."

INSTEAD OF:

Introducing someone as your "single friend,"

HOW ABOUT:

Introducing him as your friend.

INSTEAD OF:

Asking what she wants to do with the rest of her life,

HOW ABOUT:

Asking what she enjoys. Ask (and you may need to help her answer) how God has uniquely designed her, and how she might begin to explore that vocation today.

INSTEAD OF:

Homing in on accolades and accomplishments,

HOW ABOUT:

Reflecting valuable parts of his character and how you see God at work in his story.

INSTEAD OF:

Wearing a mentor mask,

HOW ABOUT:

Being yourself. Whether you're having a bad day or you just got a promotion, say so. Acting like you have it all together is less helpful than being authentic. Expose areas in which you're wrestling or ways in which God is growing you.

If you're married,

INSTEAD OF:

Saying you remember "exactly how it felt to be single,"

HOW ABOUT:

Being sympathetic, but letting the person have his own story. Your story isn't everyone else's. And because you're married, your story is automatically filtered through a different lens from that of a single person.

Also if you're married,

INSTEAD OF:

Inflating your place as a married person (making statements like "Once you're married, maybe you'll understand."),

HOW ABOUT:

Talking about your life in honest, transferrable terms—what's fun, what's challenging, what you're learning from God, where you feel He's being silent.

INSTEAD OF:

Assuming gaining ground with this age-stage is always about speaking their language and being in their world,

HOW ABOUT:

Asking if they would ever want to meet at your workplace or, if you're married, join you and your spouse/family for a meal or night out.

INSTEAD OF:

Assuming college-aged people have "so much free time,"

HOW ABOUT:

Asking if they are interested in helping out. They most likely have jobs, friends, parents, and interests beyond volunteering toward your needs. Explore what they're passionate about, and help them find outlets accordingly.

INSTEAD OF:

Pitying single people because they're single,

HOW ABOUT:

Rejoicing with them in their joys and weeping with them in their sorrows. Not all single people wish they were married, and they may be living so by choice. They may be legitimately happy, content with themselves, their community, and their freedoms.

INSTEAD OF:

Assuming all singles live a road-tripping life that involves pulling all-nighters and sleeping until noon,

HOW ABOUT:

Meeting individuals where they are, respecting that most have important jobs and live lives not unlike those of married twentysomethings.

INSTEAD OF:

Slapping on Scripture like Proverbs 31 or "If you just delight yourself in the Lord, He'll give you the desires of your heart" like a Band-Aid (which is code for "If you'd just delight better, you wouldn't be single. You're doing something wrong that's causing your singleness."),

HOW ABOUT:

Exploring the person's desires and what it means to be a godly man or woman, or what it truly means to delight in the Lord. God can handle the rest.

INSTEAD OF:

Assuming there's something romantic going on between all guy and girl friends,

HOW ABOUT:

Exploring healthy relationships between them. We've dichotomized male-female constructs to the degree that guys and girls have lost understandings of what it means to healthily be friends with the opposite sex.

INSTEAD OF:

Praying solely that your single friends would find spouses,

HOW ABOUT:

Praying for single people to continue discovering who God has made them to be and for the grace and courage to become that.

Notes

1. Abbie Smith, *Can You Keep Your Faith in College?* (Colorado Springs: Multnomah, 2006).

2. Danielle Zielinski, "Congressional Candidates Take Campaigns to Facebook, MySpace," America.gov, August 13, 2008, www.america.gov/st/elections08-english/2008/August/200808121727 44hmnietsua0.8840906.html.

3. Ken Ham, Britt Beemer, and Todd Hillard, *Already Gone: Why Your Kids Will Quit Church and What You Can Do to Stop It* (Green Forest, AR: New Leaf Publishing Group/Master Books), 2009.

4. "Most Twentysomethings Put Christianity on the Shelf Following Spiritually Active Teen Years," The Barna Group, September 11, 2006, http://www.barna.org/barna-update/article/16-teensnextgen/147-most-twentysomethings-put-christianity-on-the-shelf-following-spiritually-active-teen-years.

5. Research from Rusty Benson, "Keeping Faith from Fraying," *Center for Parent/Youth Understanding: College Transition Initiative,* http://afajournal.org/0607cti.asp (accessed October 1, 2008); Kara Powell, Cheryl Crawford, and Brad Griffin,

"You Make the Call," *Fuller Youth Institute: College Transition Initiative,* http://fulleryouthinstitute.org/2007/10/you-make-the-call/ (accessed October 18, 2008); "LifeWay Research Uncovers Reasons 18 to 22 Year Olds Drop Out of Church," *LifeWay Research,* http://www.lifeway.com/lwc/article_main_page/0%2C1703%2CA%25253D165949%252526M%25253D200906%2C00.html (accessed October 1, 2008).

6. Your capacities for wonder are obviously different from mine, but what would it look like to reignite an area of magic or imagination in your life today? Maybe go hiking, ride a motorcycle, watch kids at a playground, rent an animated film, flip through an old picture album, write a letter to your five-year-old self (or through five-year-old eyes to yourself now). The possibilities are endless, and I'm convinced that God will still want to surprise you with something new and wondrous, no matter what path you move toward. But just for a moment, a couple of hours, or even a full day, how might you recapture lost wonder in your story?

7. Philippians 1:6 (NIV)

8. The Greek verb used for "neglect" here is *kataleipo* (kat-al-i'-po), meaning "to depart from, leave behind, forsake, cease to care for, or abandon."

9. "Pure and undefiled religion in the sight of our God and Father is this: to visit orphans and widows in their distress, and to keep oneself unstained by the world" (James 1:27 NASB).

10. Colossians 1:28; Ephesians 4:11–15; Philippians 1:6.

11. Another implication of this decision was that I now had to help the older believers understand the issues these college-aged people were facing. These thoughts ended up coming together in my

book *College Ministry 101: A Guide to Working with 18–25 Year Olds* (Grand Rapids, MI: Zondervan/Youth Specialties, 2009).

12. For a full description of what this looks like, I'd recommend you read *Think Orange* by Reggie Joiner (Colorado Springs: David C. Cook, 2009).

Also from Reggie Joiner and David C.Cook:

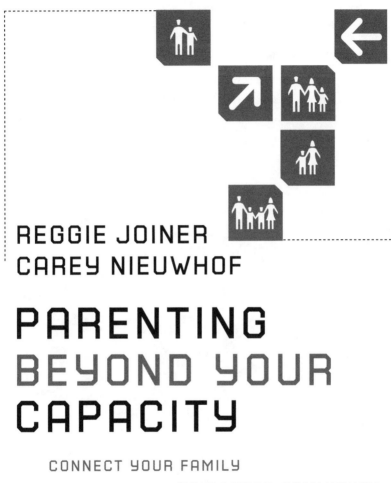

REGGIE JOINER
CAREY NIEUWHOF

PARENTING BEYOND YOUR CAPACITY

CONNECT YOUR FAMILY
TO A WIDER COMMUNITY

CHAPTER THREE ↑

Family Value #1: Widen the Circle

Pursue strategic relationships for your kids.

If you understand the physics behind using a lever of any kind, you have a visual of what it means to do something beyond your capacity. A lever enables you to move or lift something that would ordinarily exceed your ability. The word *lever* comes from a French word that means "to raise." When you use a lever, you typically exert whatever force you can on your end of the lever, and this effort magnifies energy on the other end. Basically you do your part, and the lever enhances your influence to make a greater impact.

Imagine for just a moment that you have three levers you could move to elevate the influences that affect your child's life. Suppose each lever has a different function, but they are all extremely important to the future of your son or daughter. Collectively the

Imagine for just a moment that you have three levers you could move to elevate the influences that affect your child's life.

levers represent the primary influences that will determine how your children see themselves, how they view the world, how they make decisions, how they relate to people. These levers can ultimately affect the direction of your children's lives. Although you don't have the capacity to directly impact everything that happens to your child, you do have the capacity to do your part, to apply energy to your side of the lever.

The Three Levers

In the coming chapters we will talk about the lever you use to *enhance your child's relationship with you.* At times you are sensitive enough to know that your kids need more of your attention. So you leverage your time with them. This happens when you make it a priority to be physically and emotionally present. It also is a result of communicating consistently with your children in a way that fights for their hearts. When you create a rhythm and use teachable moments to speak into their lives, you are leveraging your relational experiences to bond and build memories that fuel their emotions. When you manage this lever, you ensure that there will be a quantity of quality times in your home that will build a lasting friendship and a healthy relationship between you and your children.

The second lever is in some ways even more critical than the first. If you want to tap into unlimited capacity, you use whatever human ability you have to move this lever. It is the lever that *advances your child's relationship with God.* No one has the potential to move this lever like you do. As the parent, you are the one who can monitor their hearts, their character, and their faith. You are also the one who has the best potential to model what the unconditional love of a heavenly Father looks like. When you activate this lever, you nudge them toward their own relationship with a God who has an unlimited capacity to love them. As you apply this lever you recognize that their relationship with God is even more important than their relationship with you. You are guiding them toward an eternal relationship that will give them the ability to navigate through an uncertain future with hope.

There is also a third lever. It is similar to the first two in that it has to do with a key relationship as well. As your children get older, this lever becomes more and more important. Some experts even suggest that during the teenage years, this third one may be the best one you can leverage to influence their direction. As your direct personal influence with your children evolves in late adolescence, this lever becomes increasingly important. This chapter is about the lever that *connects your child to relationships with those outside your home.*

The importance of this third lever became very evident to me (Reggie) when my son, Reggie Paul, turned sixteen. As father and son we had always had a positive relationship, significant moments together, and lots of conversations about faith. He was integrally involved with our church. But somewhere during his second year of high school, things began to change.

As he shifted toward a certain group of friends and became more independent, he and I were both taken by surprise at the strain that began to show up in our relationship. We were going through a real tug-of-war, and it was all connected to—you might guess—a girl he was dating.

I remember thinking his years of experience with me as his father would make him pay more attention to me than to a girl he *just met*. But I was wrong. I couldn't compete. It all exploded one night when he came home past curfew, and I walked into his room to confront him.

I said, "You are late coming home from a date, and I just need to know what's going on."

He replied, "Dad, I don't really want to talk to you about it."

"Well, you don't have an option," I explained. "I need you to tell me everything that went on tonight, and I need you to tell me now."

He looked at me as if I were a stranger and said, "No. I'm not going to tell you that."

Then I did something that came naturally. I moved the first lever and said, "RP, this is me. You know I care about you. I need you to tell me what's going on because I am your father."

Then he said something that caught me off guard. None of my children had ever said it before. It was gutsy. It was honest. But it shocked me. "No, you don't understand, Dad. I'm not going to tell you *because* you are my father. You make the rules."

I just wasn't ready for that response. I was flustered. I didn't know what to do. That night I told my wife, Debbie, "If he can't talk to me because I make the rules, then I am not sure I want to make the rules anymore."

The next day, I showed up at my friend Andy Stanley's office and said, "I just don't understand. I'm trying to get my son to tell me what's going on, and he won't tell me anything."

Andy thought for a second, then with a twitch of sarcasm said to me, "Well, did *you* tell *your* father everything?"

I muttered, "No, but what does that have to do with anything?"

The next day I went back to Reggie Paul. I said, "Andy told me that you ought to tell me everything you're doing because that's what a good son would do."

No, actually, that's not what I said. I said, "I talked to Andy, and he said he didn't tell his father everything either, and I should understand why you won't tell me everything. I'm trying to be okay with that. But I do need to ask you a different question." It was then that I learned for the first time the power of the third lever. I asked my son, "If you won't tell me, then who will you tell?"

His response was easy. He said, "That's fair. I'll tell you who. I'll talk to Kevin." As soon as he said Kevin's name, I felt a huge sense of relief because Kevin had been a family friend for years. I knew he loved our family, respected me, and had the same values we had. I remember thinking that Kevin would be a very safe place to go.

I knew then more than ever before what a gift it was for me to have this other adult in my son's life. I didn't worry about what Kevin would tell Reggie Paul because I knew he would be saying the same kinds of things that I would say.

Let's rewind the conversation back to the second day in my son's bedroom to when I asked him, "If you won't tell me, then who will you tell?" What if there had not been a Kevin in his life? What if at this defining moment the best he could give me was a shrugged shoulder or an "I don't know"?

I am fortunate to have participated in a church for most of my life where it is easy to move the third lever, where men and

When you ask, "Who are you going to talk to?" would your kids have a name?

women invest in the lives of kids and teenagers because they believe it is important to widen the circle.

What if you were to have a conversation with your teenage son or daughter? When you ask, "Who are you going to talk to?" would your kids have a name? Would they identify a trusted adult in their lives who would give them a safe place to wrestle with difficult issues?

Regardless of your stage of parenting, I can promise you one thing:

A time will come when you and your children
will need another adult in their lives besides you.

We encourage parents to start moving a lever to widen the circle as soon as they can. We train church leaders to organize their ministries to put small-group leaders in the lives of kids as early as preschool. Why? Because we want to make sure parents recognize the value of having other trusted leaders in the lives of their kids as they grow up.

It is easy for us to send the wrong signals to our children when they need objective voices in their lives. The more I thought about what Reggie Paul said to me that day, the more it made sense.

He had a reason when he said, "I'm not going to tell you *because* you are my father. You make the rules." He was not simply imply-ing that he was worried about what I would do if I found out. It goes deeper than that. Other things were playing out in his mind as a sixteen-year-old. It was as if he was saying, "You are too close, you care too much, you are too connected to me. There is the potential with this issue that you could be more emotional than reasonable. You can't be as rational as you need to be, and the reason you can't is because I am your son and you are my dad. I need someone at this moment with a different kind of objectivity."

He needed more than a PARENT. He needed somebody who cared about him but who was not responsible for him. He needed somebody who would say what I would say as his parent but who didn't make the rules.

He needed more than a COMPANION his own age. He needed someone who had been down that road and could look back and say, "You need to watch out for *this* and make sure you go *that* direction."

Sometimes moving this lever can be difficult for a parent. I know I have learned a couple of really important things.

First of all, *don't take it too personally.*

You need to accept that you will not always be the one your children run to. As a matter of fact, if you try too hard to be that person, you might be the one they run away from.

Second, *don't be too proud.*

An element of this makes every parent a little nervous. I'm no different. The idea that our kids will confide in someone else about what's going on in their heads is one thing. The possibility they might get honest about what's going on in their homes could be embarrassing to me personally. Give your kids permission to express themselves in a safe place, even if it's a little awkward for you as a parent. It would be better for someone who cares about your family to have insider information than someone who doesn't. Choose to be more concerned about what your kids need as your children than about how you look as a parent.

Here's the main question: *What are you doing to encourage your child's relationships with people outside the home?* This is a powerful principle that we cannot miss as parents.

When I hear people talk about Deuteronomy 6, they often rush right by something important at the beginning. It's in the phrase, "*Hear, O Israel.*" It's what I would call the covert context of the passage. Moses is speaking to *all* of Israel about the importance of families passing on their faith to the next generation. He was talking to every parent *and* everyone else. We assume because there is so much language about family and children that he was talking primarily to parents, but Moses was speaking to *all* of Israel. The culture of the Israelites was that of a community. Not only were parents listening, but there were others in the crowd as well: aunts, uncles, grandparents, and a wider circle of adults.

The Hebrew culture described in Deuteronomy naturally promoted this kind of relationship. We're challenged to rethink our understanding of family, as the Fuller Youth Institute explains: "A family in the Old Testament would have included parents, children, workers, perhaps adult siblings with their own spouses and children. In fact, households could be compiled of as many as eighty people. These texts, such as Deuteronomy 6, are discussing the communal raising of children. Our own cultural distance from these passages may cause us to put undue pressure on parents alone."[1]

The family unit then was not always as neatly defined as we sometimes think. Regardless of how you would describe that ancient system, one thing is definitely true: The system offered significant multigenerational support for parents. I think the reason Moses would say things about "you, your children and their children after them"[2] is because all those generations were represented in the crowd.

How do we rediscover the principle of wider-circle community that existed in the Hebrew story? How do we rally parents and churches to see how strategic they are in nurturing the hearts of children?

As a parent, I believe that one of the greatest values of the church is its potential to provide community for my children. I want my children and teenagers to know that the church is a place where they can show up and be safe, a place where they can have meaningful dialogue with another trusted adult, and a place where they can ask difficult questions.

Widening the circle involves pursuing strategic relationships for your son or daughter.

In a culture where community is not automatic and there are limited role models, parents should become intentional about finding spiritual leaders and mentors for their kids. Every son and daughter needs other adults in their lives who will say things that reflect what a parent would say. One of the smartest things moms and dads can do is to participate in a church where they can find the right kind of adult influences for their kids.

Here is a piece of research that might interest some of you as parents:

> Teens who had at least one adult from church
> make a significant time investment in their lives
> … were more likely to keep attending church.
> More of those who stayed in church—by a

margin of 46 percent to 28 percent—said five
or more adults at church had invested time
with them personally and spiritually.[3]

I have observed a lot of teenagers. From the time they hit middle school, they start moving away from home. They are not doing anything wrong; it's just the way they are made. They are becoming independent, and they begin redefining themselves through the eyes of other people who are not in their immediate family.

The older they get, the more important it is for them to have other voices in their lives saying the same things but in a different way. Teenage sons and daughters need to have other voices speaking into their worlds.

Parents who do not understand this principle have forgotten what it was like to be a teenager. I cannot count the times my kids would quote something a teacher, our student pastor, or a coach had said. They would act like it was the first time they had ever heard it. I wanted to blurt out, "I have been telling you that for sixteen years!" They were hearing it in a different way because they were at a different stage, and they just needed a different voice.

Widening the circle transitions your child from a "me" approach to a "we" approach.

When you widen the circle, you not only recognize the need for others to influence your children but also the need for your children to be a part of something that is much larger than just your family. A wider circle gives them not only a place to belong, but a significant role to engage in the bigger story we talked about in the last chapter.

Seth Godin makes this observation: "Human beings can't help it; we need to belong. One of the most powerful of our survival mechanisms is to be part of a tribe, to contribute to (and take from) a group of like-minded people."[4]

Don't miss this point. The right community is not only important because of what it gives to your children, but also

> **The right community is not only important because of what it gives to your children, but also because of what it requires from your children.**

because of what it requires from your children. Children need more than just a family that gives them unconditional acceptance and love; they need a tribe that gives them a sense of belonging and significance. The concept of church in the New Testament was never intended to simply be something your children attend. Church should be defined as a vibrant community that engages your children to demonstrate God's love to a broken world. When parents and leaders synchronize around this aspect of a wider circle, it has the potential to mobilize a child's faith from something that is static to something that is dynamic.

In *Inside Out Families*, Diana Garland reports on her study of what makes the most impact in a student's spiritual life. She concludes after extensive surveys and research, "Community service was significantly more closely related to the faith development of teens than attending worship services. Service appears to be more powerful than Sunday school, Bible study, or participation in worship in the faith development of teenagers."[5]

She goes on to document that when teens serve alongside adults, the experience broadens their faith and redefines their understanding of church.

We recently asked a group of seasoned leaders from around the country this question about spiritual development: "If you had six ninth-grade boys or girls for four years, what would you do to encourage their spiritual development?" They each talked about different work projects and mission endeavors. Some mentioned the amount of time they would devote to building the relationship. Some brought up authors they would want to read together. Toward the end of the conversation, we realized that no one had brought up taking them to any kind of classroom presentation. Although these leaders guide churches with a large array of programs, not one suggested just putting teens into classes or trying to simply get them to attend church. Instinctively, many leaders recognize something more relational and experiential required for spiritual formation. What if *that's* the kind of experience that student ministries facilitated for kids? What if that's what church became for young people?

Actually the approach they described seemed similar to what Jesus did with His twelve disciples over two thousand years ago. Jesus did not teach the disciples to do ministry. He did ministry with the disciples while He taught them.

Something powerful happens when you partner with other influences who desire to instill a sense of mission into the hearts of your children. You give them a different view of their place in the world, and you transfer a different kind of passion to them that your family alone cannot give them. It doesn't mean that you as parents can't engage in this mission with them. You should attempt to let your kids see what God can do through your family, as well as leverage influences to show them what God can do through them personally.

I (Carey) always knew there was a passage into manhood that was supposed to take place, but I had no idea how it happened. My son Jordan and I talked about it, and when he turned thirteen we set up what we refer to as his mentoring year. Early in the year, we sat down and selected five men in our relational circle that we both knew and felt comfortable with. I approached each man and explained what we were doing.

The plan was fairly simple. I asked each mentor to spend one day with Jordan over the summer. They could do whatever they wanted to do, and over the course of the day, I asked each mentor to impart one spiritual truth (something faith-based) and one life truth (good advice). I also checked calendars and made sure each mentor could make it to a dinner at my place after the summer was over.

The mentors did different things. A few took Jordan camping, and another took him to work. My friend Chuck, who is a police chaplain, took him for a ride in a cruiser and, rumor has it, locked him up in a jail cell. My dad, who immigrated to Canada in 1959 as a teenager, took him through southwestern Ontario and showed him all the places he used to work as a young man trying to make his way in a new country.

When the summer wrapped up, we gathered at our place. It was a great feast. We barbecued some steak, drank Coke, ate ice cream, and ensured there wasn't a salad in sight. It was, after all, a man's meal.

Jordan had kept a journal over the summer, and after dinner he spent some time telling each man what impacted him the most during their days together. Jordan presented each of the men with a Bible with the man's name inscribed on the cover. Each of the mentors then took a few minutes to make some remarks about Jordan and also reflected on some of the gifts they saw at work in his life.

After the men finished, we all gathered around Jordan and laid our hands on him. I read Deuteronomy 6:4–8 and spoke a few words into my son's life, and then we prayed together. Each man took his turn, and Jordan prayed as well. To say it was a powerful moment is an understatement.

As we were wrapping up that night, there wasn't a dry eye in the place. So many of the guys there that night said, "I wish someone had done that for me when I was thirteen." Five years later, I'm still amazed at the power that experience carried.

Just a few months ago, we completed the mentoring process for my younger son, Sam. He had some incredible moments with his mentors last summer, but what struck me at the celebration dinner was how much the experience had impacted the mentors themselves. In fact, the time together was so meaningful for the mentors that over dinner, John (a former pro football player) said that he'd like to gather every year with the guys (and with Sam) for a dinner, if that was okay with Sam. We're officially planning it for next year.

A wider circle has incredible benefits that run in more directions than we might suspect. It became obvious to me as a pastor that other adults could and should have significant relationships with my kids. Understanding the impact some of those mentors had in my sons' lives inspired me to work toward a ministry style that would put weekly mentors in the lives of kids and students.

About a year after Jordan's mentoring year I told the story during a message at the church I lead. People were moved, and numerous people indicated they were going to implement some type of mentoring plan with their son or daughter.

As people filed out, a single mom came to talk to me. I'll never forget Laura's words: "Carey, I love how you had the opportunity to do that with Jordan, and I'm sure it was a great experience, but you're a pastor and you're a guy. You're well-connected. You have men in your life and people around you who you can call on. I'm a single mom. I don't have those connections. Who's going to be there for my son, Aaron?"

That was a reminder of how important it is for the church and parents to partner. The reason it is important to connect with a faith community is that many are designed to encourage leaders who will actually spend time mentoring and coaching kids from all kinds of families.

Heather Zempel speaks firsthand of the impact of this kind of environment. As the minister who leads programs for spiritual growth at National Community Church in Washington DC, Heather points out the difference between a travel agent and a tour guide. A travel agent sits behind a desk and makes arrangements and gives directions. A tour guide walks along with the traveler, answering questions and prompting conversation along the way. As we widen our children's and teenagers' circles to include more tour guides and fewer travel agents, the influence of others will foster lifelong effects.[6]

Next Steps

Look for a church that values community.

Think about it as a parent. Isn't it true if you go back to your story, there is a short list of people who influenced your faith or character? If you could go back and redo your relationships as an adult, you would probably add more of some people in your life and take away some others. People influence us. Most of us can remember people who showed up at the right time, who became a needed voice to give us direction.

What if you could find a ministry or church where your son or daughter could begin developing a sense of community? A community where authentic relationships develop, relationships not only between peers but also with adult leaders. Where trust gets built and healthy friendships form. Your children need someone else to believe in them. They need a place to belong, besides home. The goal is for you to pursue strategic relationships so another adult voice will be speaking into your son's or daughter's life, saying the kinds of things you would try to say as a parent.

The goal is for you to pursue strategic relationships so another adult voice will be speaking into your son's or daughter's life, saying the kinds of things you would try to say as a parent.

Michael Ungar, a social work researcher, offers a powerful metaphor in the book *The We Generation: Raising Socially Responsible*

Kids. When parents are not available, "our kids can call for roadside service to get a boost when their emotional batteries go dead." In these times, "other adults can play the roles of mirrors and mentors. Mirrors are people who reflect back to our children their importance. Mentors show our children how to be their best."[7]

A growing number of churches are establishing ministries that prioritize the idea of building community. Even if they have larger group gatherings and other programs, they have a goal to put consistent, trusted adults in the lives of kids and teenagers. One of the most effective ways to build community is through a small group with leaders who get to know the kids and their parents.

Small groups are just what their name implies: a gathering of twelve or fewer who meet together in a group. A small group is typically not led by a traditional teacher but by a leader whose primary task is to build relationships with the kids he or she leads. As kids move into middle and high school, having the same leader in their lives for multiple years can be even more beneficial. The goal is to develop a graduated system where your son or daughter would have consistent leaders with whom they can develop trusted relationships.

Work with other leaders to find opportunities for your kids to serve.

Did you know there is something more important than getting your kids to simply go to church on Sunday mornings? By helping them find opportunities to serve others, you'll encourage them to *be* the church instead of just going to church.

It is too easy for us to find a false sense of security in the notion that our children are growing because they attend something. When we started our churches, we both adopted systems where high school students served on Sunday mornings and had their own small-group time in the afternoon. These students were given several options to serve the church during the morning time, from teaching younger children to working on technical teams to greeting visitors at the door.

Several parents became concerned when we moved teenagers out of Sunday morning classes to this Sunday afternoon group model. They had been programmed, like most parents, to believe that the faith development of their teenagers could happen only in a Sunday morning Sunday school class. No wonder so many of our students graduate from high school and drop out of church. They were never given the opportunity to be the church while they were growing up in church. When parents and leaders work together to encourage students in ministry, a stronger faith is forged.

I (Reggie) told you earlier about how my friend Kevin was a life-changing influence as my son's small-group leader. Kevin tells about how his own son, Brock, has embraced the opportunity to serve. As a high school junior, Brock leads a small group of third-grade boys on Sunday morning. How influential is a high school junior for eight-year-olds? Think high school superhero. Kevin recently saw those third graders show up at Brock's varsity basketball

Don't underestimate what serving inside the church, in your community, and even globally can do to the heart of your son or daughter.

game. They were Brock's biggest fans, not just because he swished a three-pointer, but because he was making a difference in the lives of these younger kids. So if you are Brock's parent, what do you think is more important? That he's sitting in a class, or that Brock's having an experience that is transforming his faith and character?

Don't underestimate what serving inside the church, in your community, and even globally can do to the heart of your son or daughter. We even know some parents and leaders who strive to make sure their teenagers are involved in at least one overseas mission effort before they graduate. They understand how the experience of personal ministry can affect someone's sense of purpose. It is not enough to tell children they are significant. Most of our children will never really believe they are significant until we give them something significant to do.

Search for mentors in your community.

Maybe you don't live near a church that has the kind of ministry we describe. If that's the case, whom do you know within your relational network who could be part of a wider circle? Maybe you have a friend, neighbor, grandparent, or colleague who could be a positive spiritual and moral voice in the life of your son or daughter? If so, why not begin a conversation with that person about a mentoring relationship with your child?

Whatever it takes, as parents we need to become more intentional about widening the circle. If we want to parent beyond our capacity, then we have to tap into the capacity of the faith community around us. Don't forget the color orange. It reminds you that your parenting is not enough. You need to tap into the influence of others. This is a very important value for you to embrace as a mom or dad. Even though it doesn't seem important when children are young, it's more important than it feels. Establishing the principle of community early in their lives can potentially prevent a lot of unnecessary strife later.

When you widen the circle, the goal is to have other trusted adults in the lives of children *before* they need them so they will be there *when* they need them.

When you widen the circle, the goal is to have other trusted adults in the lives of children *before* they need them so they will be there *when* they need them.

Moses passed these values along to the entire community because he knew it would take multiple influences to guard the faith of a generation.

God never intended life to be lived in isolation, and what's true of individuals is also true of families. We have been called to live as part of a much wider circle and God-engineered community to help all of us parent beyond our capacity.

Widen the Circle

DISCUSSION QUESTIONS

Continue the Conversation

Key question: *How am I connecting my child to a wider circle of influence?*

1. When you were young, was there another adult in your life (besides your parents) who gave you good advice and invested in you in a positive way? What impact did this relationship have on you?

2. Many of you did not have another adult who invested in your early years. How might your teenage years have looked different if another adult had been pouring into your life? What knowledge or values do you wish someone had instilled in you as a teenager?

3. How many trusted adults are speaking into your child or teenager's life? What fears and hopes do you have about other leaders being involved in your child or teenager's life?

4. Why does it often feel like you are flying solo as you raise your kids? What next steps could you take, or what places could you look to widen the circle for your family? How could you and your children begin to experience deeper community?

5. How does the right kind of community create a healthy environment for you to grow as an individual? Specifically, how do you see community being a benefit to your kids?

If you attend a church, start talking to your child about what happened in small group. Who are her friends? What's her small group leader's name? What did they talk about or study? Make sure to introduce yourself to your son or daughter's small group leader. Brainstorm with your child ways to get to know the leader better, like going out for ice cream or having the leader over for a family lunch. (If you are not part of a church that offers community to you and your child, we recommend www.OrangeParents.com for churches in your area.)

Read Deuteronomy 5:1.

Moses summoned all Israel and said:

Hear, O Israel, the decrees and laws I declare in your hearing today. Learn them and be sure to follow them.

Read Deuteronomy 6:4.

Hear, O Israel: The LORD our God, the LORD is one.

Read Deuteronomy 6:5–7.

Love the LORD your God with all your heart and with all your soul and with all your strength. These commandments that I give you today are to be upon your hearts. Impress them on your children.

Remember when Moses gave this speech, and imagine being gathered with the Israelites for the talk. Imagine hearing that talk as a parent—would it come as good news, or would you feel overwhelmed? Why?

REFLECT: Imagine hearing the message as someone without kids. If you were a mentor or significant voice in the life of someone else's child or teenager, what could you do to develop a stronger relationship with that child? How would you talk to him or her about faith? How would you develop a trusted friendship with the parents?

XP3

COLLEGE

A resource to equip small group leaders and mentors
and help you stop the slow fade

www.XP3College.org

orange

ORANGE IS A UNIQUE STRATEGY FOR
COMBINING THE CRITICAL INFLUENCES
IN LIFE TO FUEL FAITH IN THE NEXT
GENERATION

IT'S A STRATEGY THAT SYNCHRONIZES THE INFLUENCE OF PARENTS AND CHURCH LEADERS TOWARD A COMPREHENSIVE PLAN FROM PRESCHOOL TO COLLEGE

FIRST LOOK PRESCHOOL CURRICULUM
252 BASICS CHILDREN'S CURRICULUM
XP3 STUDENT CURRICULUM

THINK ORANGE PUBLISHED MATERIALS
ORANGE LEADERS TRAINING RESOURCES
ORANGE CONFERENCE & TOUR
ORANGE PARENTS RESOURCES

CAMP KIDJAM
AMBER SKY MUSIC

www.OrangeThinkers.com

leaders

Orange Leaders is an online curriculum that provides training materials for leaders and volunteers in every age-group ministry. Learn with other leaders through the blog, discussion board, or podcasts, all free. Additionally, subscribe to the Orange Leaders Curriculum to receive monthly training modules for ministry leaders and volunteers.

Learn more at www.OrangeLeaders.com

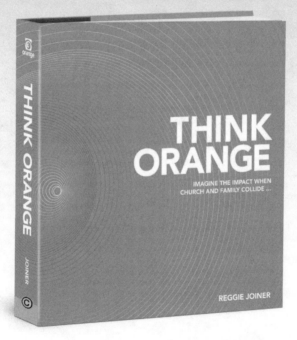